CHAPTER 1

Portrait photography overview

Portraiture has a long history dating back to pre-historic times. Photography has been used for portraiture since the middle of the 19th century when daguerreotypes became popular with educated middle-class citizens because they were excitingly new and accessible. In contrast, the upper classes retained their traditional preferences for oil paintings.

Busy people found the combination of relatively short sitting times and lower overall costs of a daguerreotype irresistible. Interestingly, silver halide photography, which evolved at the same time, had the advantage of being infinitely reproducible – and both safer and cheaper. Early portrait photographers like Julia Margaret Cameron and Edward S. Curtis gained prominence in the 19th century, followed by Philippe Halsman, Dorothea Lange, Richard Avedon and Arnold Newman as well as the many less-famous photographers who worked for the movie studios during the 20th century. Each worked within the constraints of the equipment and social mores of their times, documenting both famous people and relative unknowns.

It's worth looking through collections of photographs from these accomplished portraitists as they can still provide inspiration today. Fortunately today's cameras and media are much simpler to use so it's a lot easier to achieve the outcomes you want.

In essence, portrait photography usually concentrates upon subjects' faces and photographers aim to capture the subject's distinguishing features, often in the most flattering light. Good portraits also record aspects of the subject's identity, attitude ('poise' or discomfiture) and personality.

Portraits can range from extreme close-ups showing part of the face to shots that encompass the subject's entire body. Some portraits go even further and present the subject in an environment that 'says' something about them to the viewer. It all depends on how the project is approached.

In this pocket guide we outline the factors you need to consider when preparing for a portrait photo shoot.

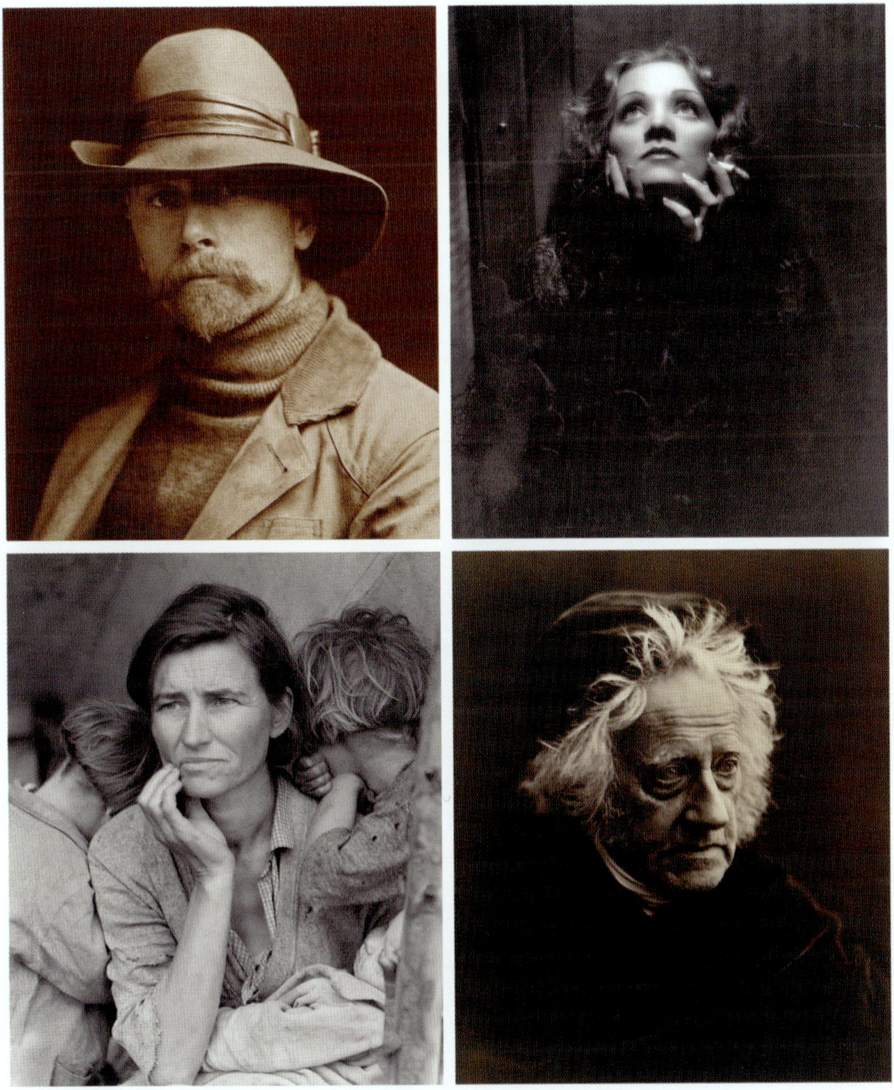

Four examples of classical portraiture from the past: clockwise from top left: Edward S. Curtis – Self portrait. Published in 1910 (possibly earlier); Don English (1901-1964); Publicity photo of Marlene Dietrich for the film Shanghai Express (1932); Sir John Herschel (1815-1879), photographed by Julia Margaret Cameron in April 1867; Dorothea Lange (1895-1965) – Migrant Mother, Nipomo, California.

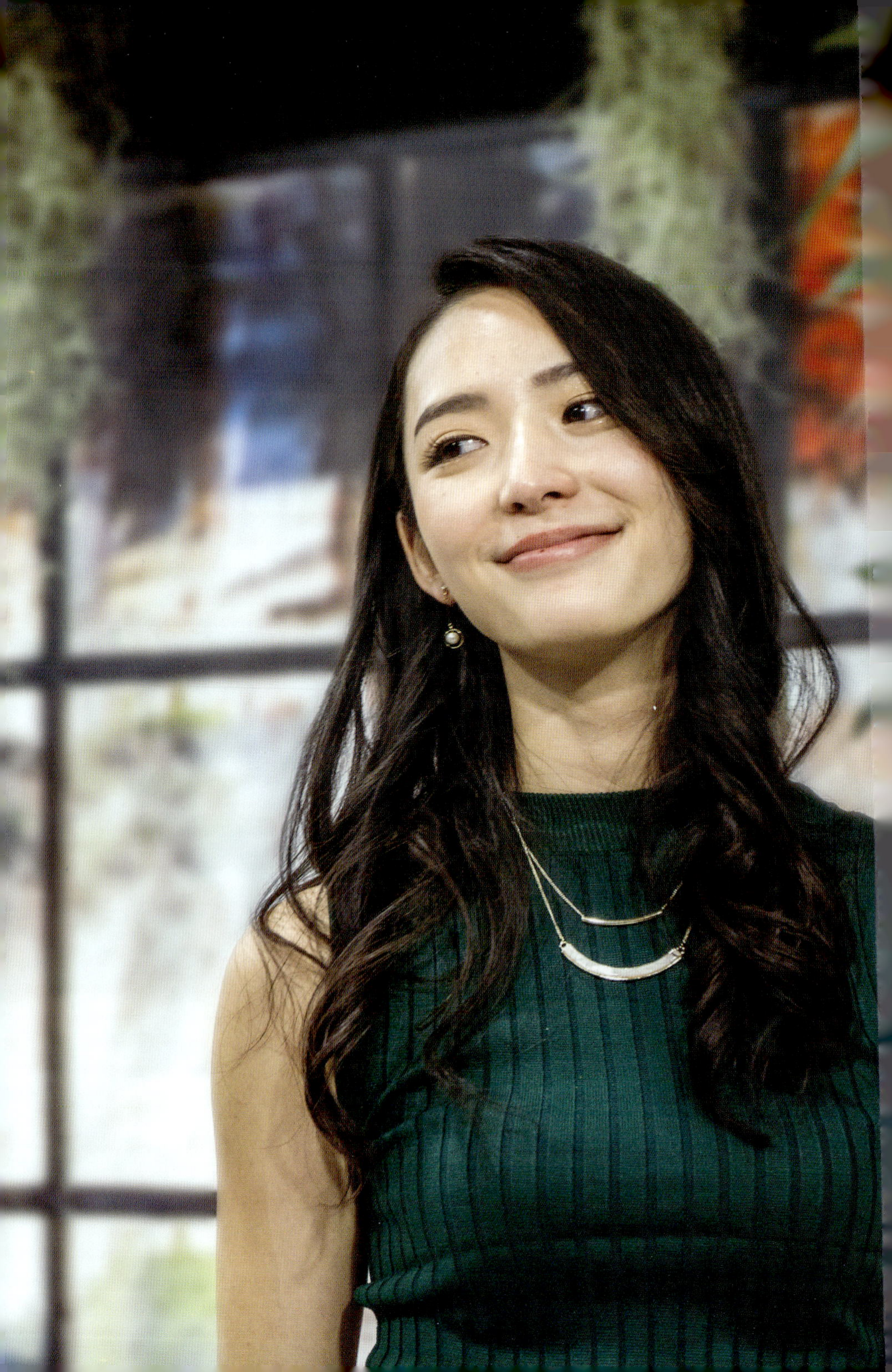

We also look at the equipment you need and provide advice on shooting techniques for different situations, starting with some very basic decisions that will affect your approach and the results you obtain.

Single or groups?

Different issues arise when shooting portraits of just one subject and taking group portraits. Single shots only require one person to co-operate with the photographer, while with group portraits the photographer is expected to have everybody looking at their best. This can be tough as anyone who has photographed a family or group of friends will testify. It's difficult to ensure that everyone in the group has their eyes open and is looking at the camera – or in a direction the photographer indicates. We deal with this topic in detail in Chapter 6.

Formal or candid?

Portrait photography can be split into two main categories: format and candid. In the former, the subject deliberately 'sits' for the photographer; in the latter,

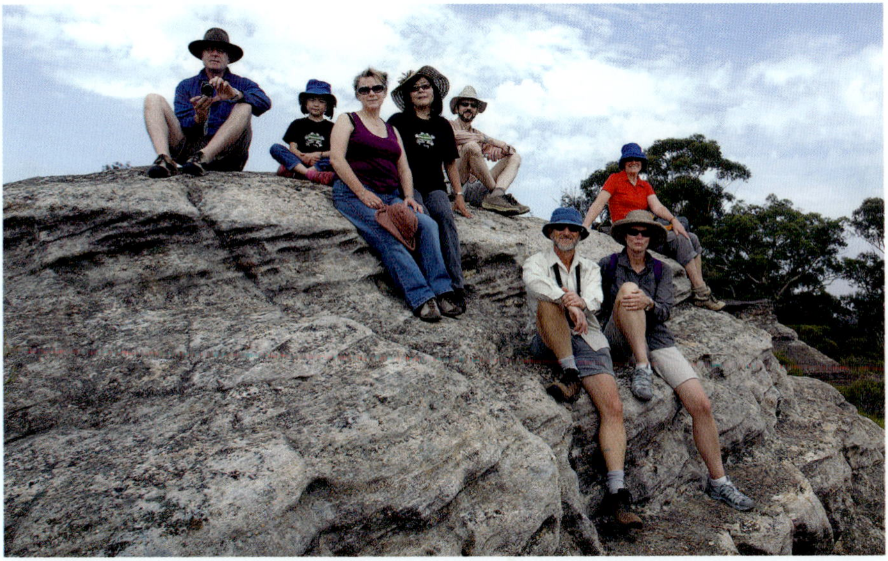

Left: Taking portrait shots of just one person is relatively easy when they are happy and relaxed. Above: Natural lighting is usually the best for group portraits especially in attractive environments.

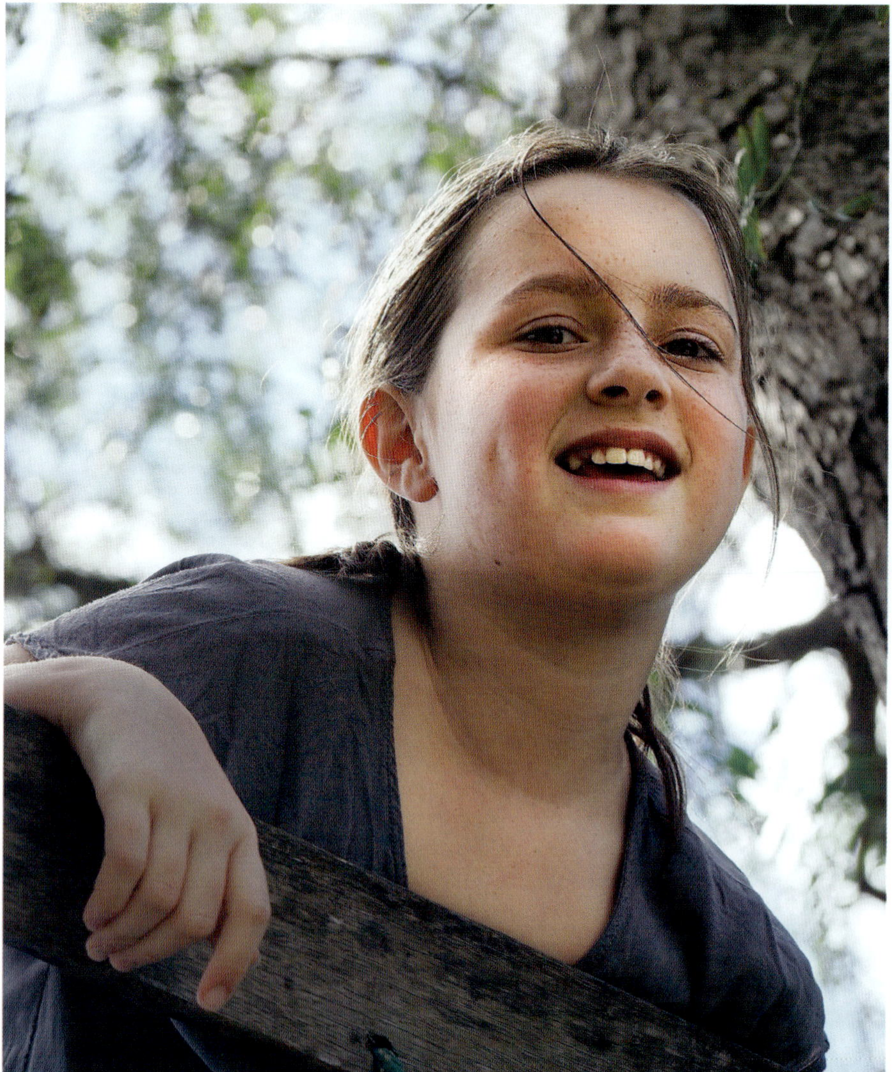

Even a casual snapshot can make an attractive portrait if it records a spontaneous moment.

subjects are usually unaware of being photographed. Both are valid – although quite different – approaches and both require different shooting techniques.

Formal portraits are often shot in studio environments with artificial lighting. They rely on the photographer establishing a connection with the subject to put them at ease before any shots are taken. This often requires prior research into the subject and their requirements and interests.

Lighting in formal portraits is always carefully planned, even when artificial lights aren't used. While 'environmental' portraits make use of natural lighting, the photographer must manage the shoot to ensure it is soft and flattering and comes from the right direction.

Candid portraits usually require the subject to be unaware they are being photographed, which means the photographer must strive to be inconspicuous. If subjects are aware of the photographer, they shouldn't consciously react or 'perform' for the camera.

When shooting candid portraits, photographers are constrained by the ambient lighting and must make the best of the situations they face, which can often change with weather conditions and subject movement.

This can be challenging at times and requires the photographer to have a good understanding of the range of tones the camera can record and the different ways it deals with contrasty and flat lighting.

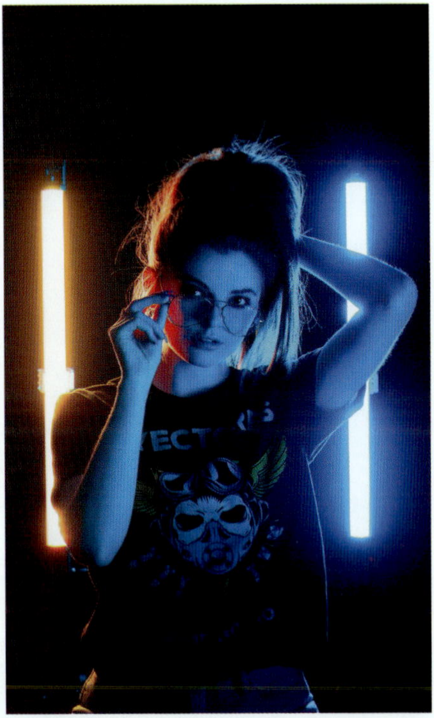

Creatively planned and positioned lighting, a defocused background and arresting pose make this formal portrait an eye-catching alternative to bland 'head shots'. (Source: Camera House.)

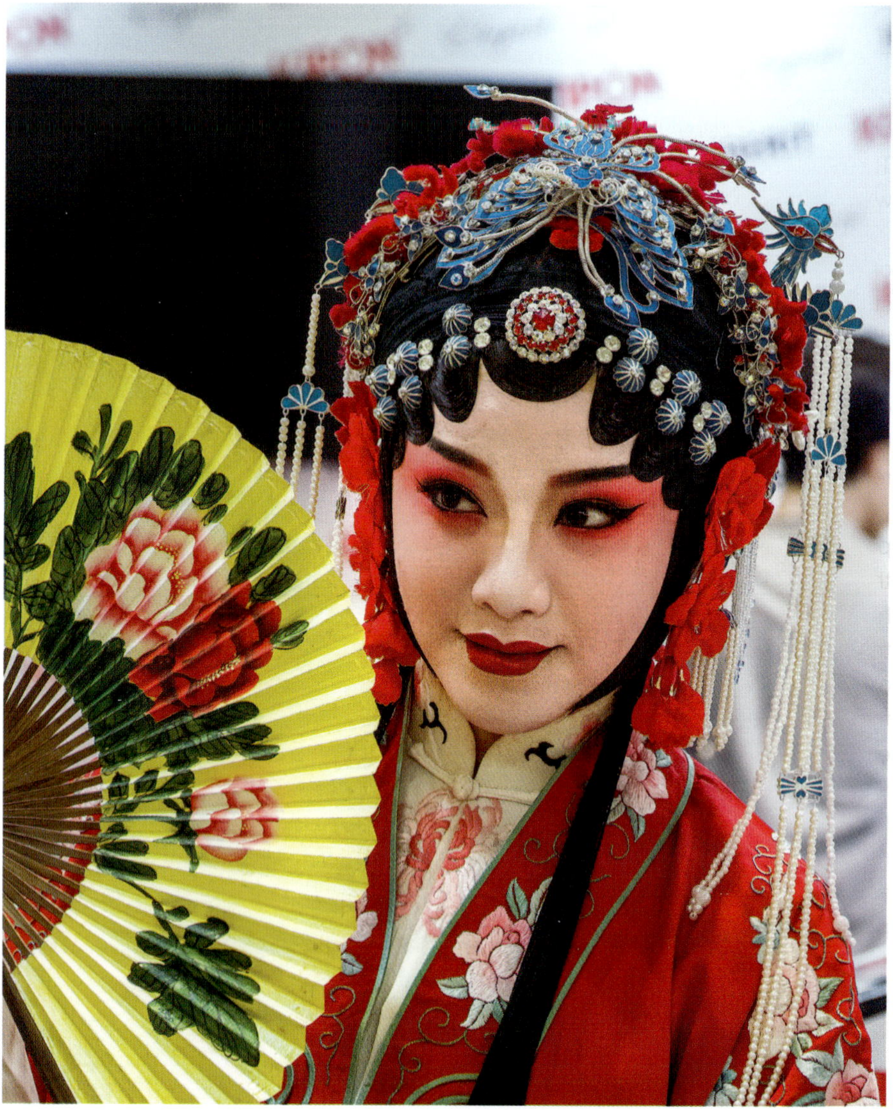

Special-purpose portraits can feature costumes, make-up and props that make them stand out against everyday snapshots. It's important to pose the subject to their best advantage, which can include careful use of accessories.

Different approaches

There are several definable approaches a photographer can take, each depending on the type of portrait that's being taken. The first step is to decide just what you want the portrait to 'say'.

Should it present a 'warts-and-all' view or does it need to be flattering? The first strategy might apply to a creative shot that aims to bring out hidden depths in the subject, while the second would definitely apply to studio portraits that will be framed or published in magazines, reports or books.

Suppose you want to create a particular 'atmosphere' for the shot that reveals a little more than a bland head-on photo. It's up to you to set the background and lighting, introduce any suitable 'props' and work with the subject to bring out the required emotion. It can be as simple and straightforward as having the subject look intently into the camera against a minimal background, or as complex as setting up a group shot that shows each person's place in an overall scheme.

Another approach aims to say more about the subject by including them in a selected environment or situation. It's important for the photographer to work with the subject and provide clear directions as to how they should pose to convey the meaning or feeling both parties want to express.

While many studio portraits still adopt the formal head and shoulders style for individual portraits or height-balanced groupings for families and other groups, an increasing number of studio clients are looking for more creative approaches. For example, a corporate portrait of an executive for an annual report might present the subject in their office or, in the case of someone like an architect, engineer or landscape designer, out on a work site. Writers are often photographed with laptops and screens against a bookcase background.

Advertising photography and fashion photography have long given full rein to creative impulses which, in turn, can trickle through to studio portraiture. Photographers at all levels can learn a lot from these popular media images. Many studios also offer 'glamour' shots or shots taken in different costumes to suit different customers' requirements.

A key factor in setting up all formal portraits involves deciding how much of the background to include and where to position the subject. Choosing appropriate 'props' also plays an important role both in categorising the subject and making them feel more relaxed for the camera.

The candid approach covers a wide range of situations from street photography, where subjects are unaware of being photographed, through to collaborative shots in which the subject knows the photographer is taking pictures but is not sure about exactly when the shutter is being released. Portraits of this type are often captured in family and social situations to show people behaving naturally or living their life uninterrupted. Paparazzi almost invariably use this approach – with or without the subject's co-operation.

Finally, creative portraiture can often go beyond an image that is 'straight out of the camera' through use of extensive editing, multiple exposures and use of techniques like High Dynamic Range (HDR) shooting and editing. Experimentation with colours and tonal reproduction also fall into this category.

Different approaches are taken for different subject types and occasions. They also vary depending on whether the portrait is of a single subject or a group – and how large that group is. Ambient conditions at the time of shooting also play a role and photographers are often required to change strategies as a result of changing weather conditions, children's behaviour and attention spans and issues with some subjects. A flexible approach is well worth developing to cope with potential problems.

Useful links

People pictures in travel photography
www.bit.ly/3MJX3Qh

A history of portrait photography
www.bit.ly/3wEaBXP

Right: Travel can provide excellent subjects for portraiture in unique environments.

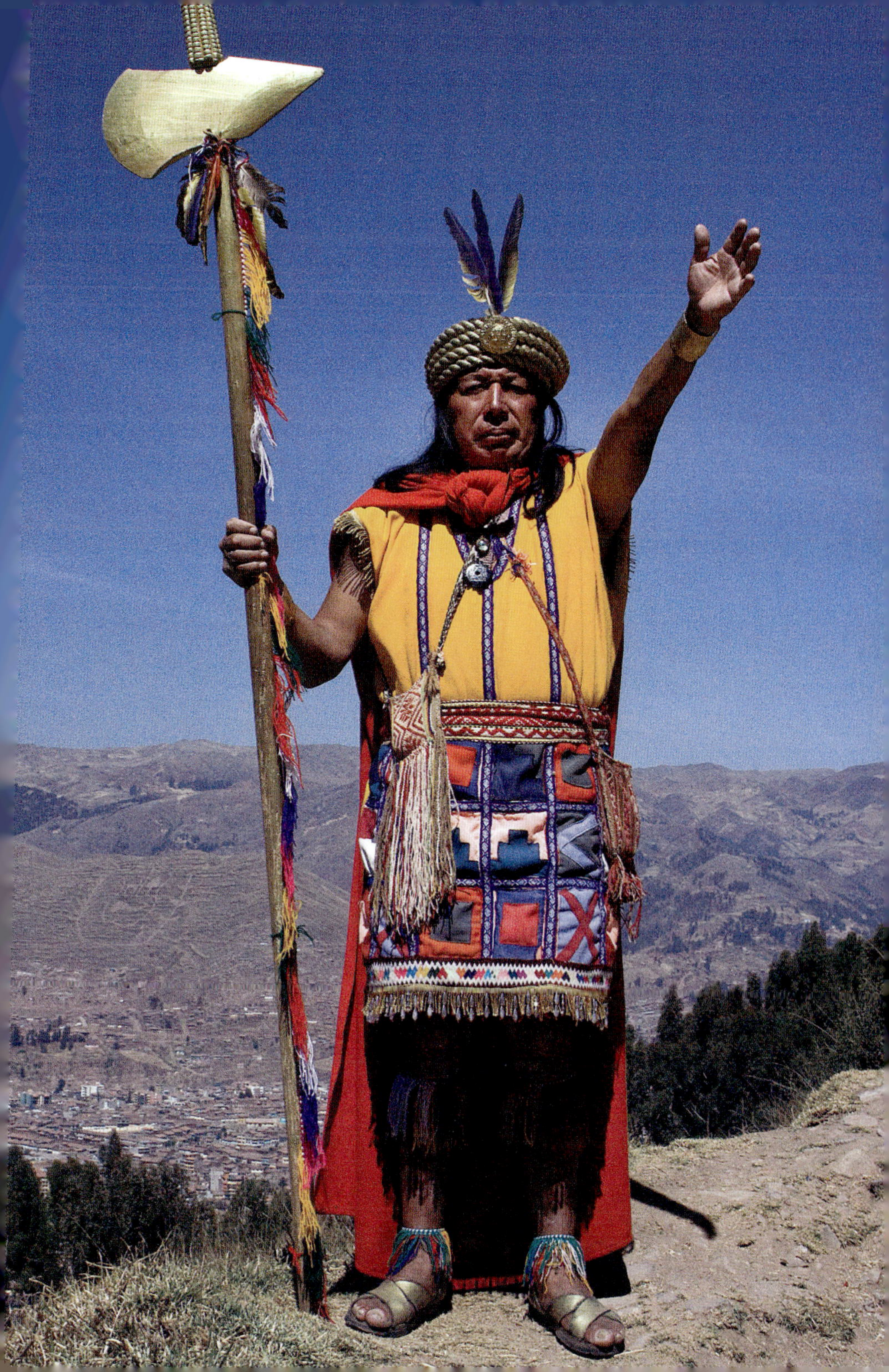

CHAPTER 2

Equipment requirements

Although portrait photos can be taken with pretty much any camera (including smartphones), interchangeable-lens cameras generally do the best job, since they let you select an appropriate lens (see below), set the optimal exposure parameters and capture raw files to ensure you have the best starting point for processing your shots. Different types of portraiture have slightly different equipment requirements, which are outlined in this chapter.

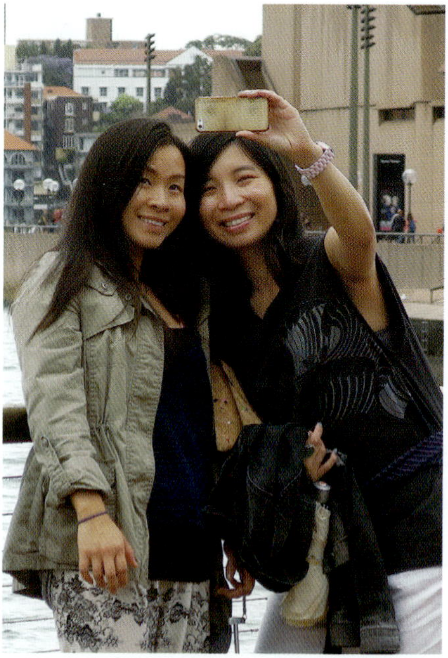

While it's easy to take quick selfies with a smartphone, especially when you are on-the-go, a 'proper' interchangeable-lens camera provides superior results for most other portraits.

While portraitists working in studio environments are able to take advantage of large, high-resolution cameras, fast lenses and expensive lighting set-ups, the majority of photographers usually find their existing equipment can deliver satisfactory results. Their images may lack the polished, professional appearance of studio shots but they're often much more engaging because they're natural-looking and provide a more 'truthful' depiction of the subject.

It doesn't really matter whether your camera is a DSLR or mirrorless model – or if it has a 'full frame', APS-C or Micro Four Thirds (M4/3) sized sensor. What matters most is your understanding of how to use it and whether you've selected the most appropriate lens and camera settings. These choices can, in fact, influence the end result more than you might initially think

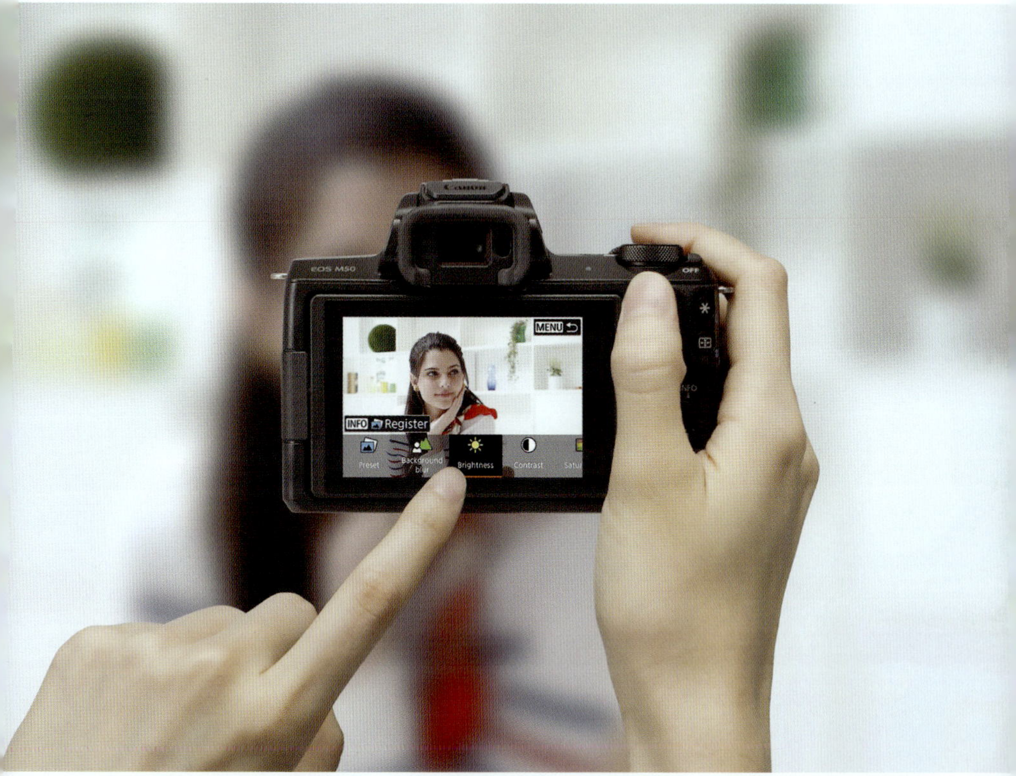

Entry-level interchangeable-lens cameras often have easy-to-use presets that let users select adjustments for background blurring, brightness and contrast via touch controls.

Know your lenses

Most people know there are two types of lenses: prime (or single focus) and zoom. Prime lenses can usually be smaller, lighter and easier to make than zoom lenses but they're generally less versatile. Zoom lenses provide versatility at the expense of lens speed and, often, size and weight.

Regardless of the type of lens, all lens designs are influenced by three factors: speed, weight and price. Designers must balance these factors to create lenses that consumers want and are prepared to buy and use. However, they are inevitably constrained by some important parameters.

Lens **'speed'** defines how quickly light can reach the image sensor. It is determined by the size of the aperture that lets the light into the camera which, in turn, is dictated by the size of the glass 'elements' that make up the lens.

The fastest lenses which have maximum apertures between f/0.95 and f/1.2 contain large elements that require a lot of heavy glass. This makes them heavy to carry; some weigh two kilograms or more.

They also cost a lot to make, which means they're even more expensive to buy. As a guide, every 1/3 of an f-stop of speed advantage you can expect **at least** a 200 gram increase in the weight of the lens and a $500 increase in its price.

Sometimes you don't want to use a very wide aperture setting. While it can make it easy to blur out distracting backgrounds, the fastest lenses also have **very** shallow planes of focus, which can make precise focusing very tricky. There are also times when it's better to stop down and reveal background details to add context to the picture.

Prime lenses for close-up portraits usually have maximum apertures between f/2.0 and f/2.8. This provides a shallow depth of focus with plenty of scope for creative background blurring. These lenses are often more affordably priced than the fastest lenses.

Zoom lenses are often a stop or two slower than primes, but they are easier to use and wide aperture settings usually produce attractive background blurring, especially at longer focal lengths so they shouldn't be seen as inferior. The highest-quality zooms have constant maximum apertures, usually around f/4 for 24-105mm zooms.

Cheaper zoom lenses have variable apertures, such as a range from f/3.5 at 24mm to f/5.6 at 105mm. Both types of zoom lenses provide photographers with plenty of scope to be creative when framing shots than prime lenses. However, the ability to blur out backgrounds at longer focal lengths is better with constant maximum aperture zooms.

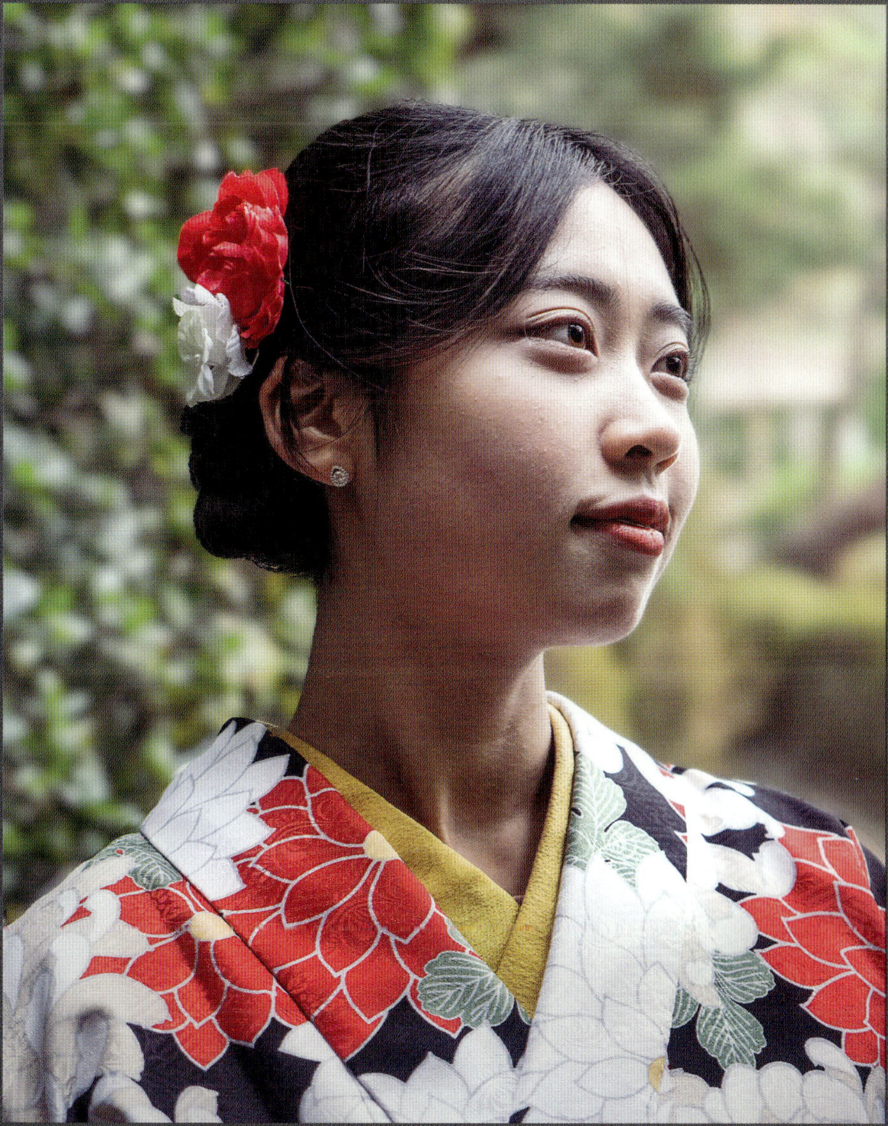

Use of a wide lens aperture – in this case, f/2.8 – produced attractive background blurring for this close-up portrait.

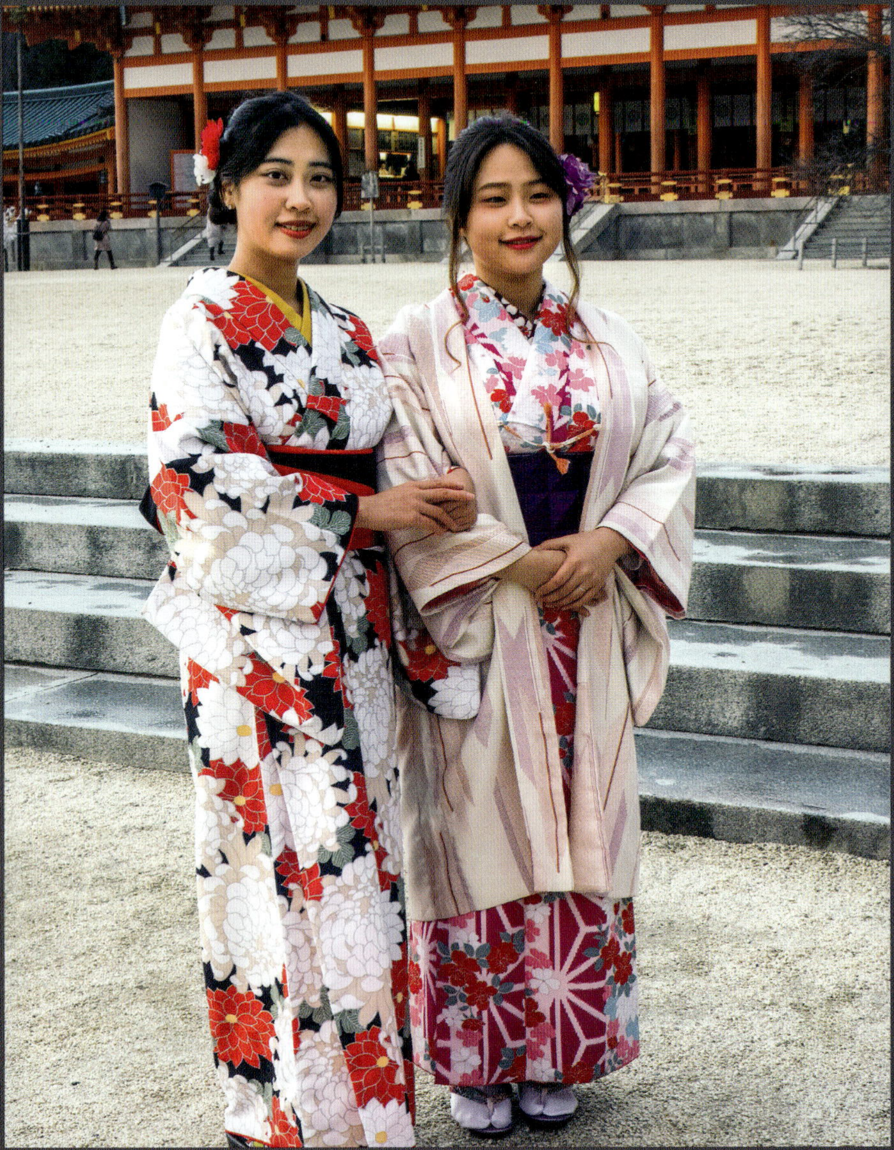

Stopping down to f/8 for a different type of portrait added meaningful context to the shot.

Lens choices

Fast telephoto lenses with moderately short focal lengths have long been the first choice of professional portrait photographers. There are two reasons behind the choice:

1. Moderate tele lenses provide a comfortable working distance between the camera and the subject, preventing the subject from feeling crowded out and overwhelmed by the presence of the photographer.

2. The short telephoto lens is considered by many professional photographers (and also equipment manufacturers) as 'ideal' for portraiture because of its flattering perspective. The most popular focal lengths lie between 85mm and 105mm in 35mm format, although this can extend to about 70mm at the shorter end or 135mm to 200mm in some situations.

3. Prime lenses are often used by studio portraitists, with fast 85mm lenses being popular for cameras that have 36 x 24 mm sensors. Fast zoom lenses are also popular with both professionals and photo enthusiasts because of their versatility.

4. Wide angle lenses are only suitable for photographing moderate-to-large groups of people. When used for individual portraits they often create unattractive distortions.

5. Photographers shooting with cropped-sensor (APS-C or Micro Four Thirds) cameras need to take account of the effective focal lengths produced by the sensor's crop factor. Most APS-C cameras have sensors measuring approximately 23.5 x 15.7 mm and a 1.5x crop factor, which means a 90mm lens covers the same angle of view as a 135mm lens on a 'full frame' camera.

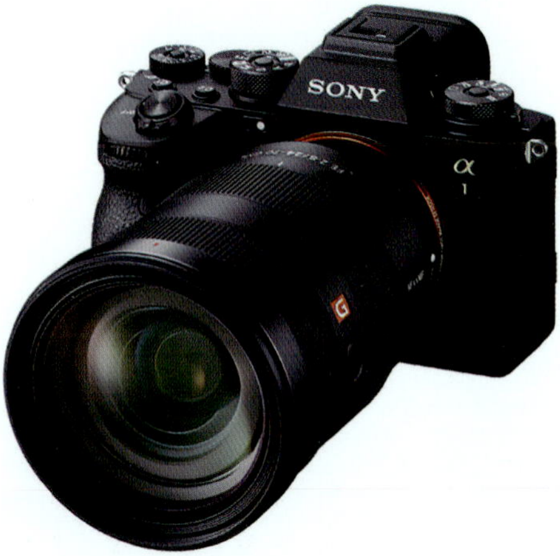

This combination of a high-resolution camera with a fast (f/2.8 constant maximum aperture) 24-70mm zoom lens allows you to take both individual and group portraits. It would be especially well suited to wedding and event photography.

Canon uses smaller sensors that measure 22.3 x 14.9 mm, which have a crop factor of 1.6x, so a 90mm lens is equivalent to a 144mm lens on a 'full frame' camera. M4/3 cameras use 17.3 x 13.0 mm sensors with a 2x crop factor so users of those cameras would find a 90mm lens has an equivalent focal length of 180mm.

Light and the inverse-square law

Before you can begin to work with light it's important to understand how it works. This is defined by the **inverse-square law**, which applies to all forms of electromagnetic radiation and explains why light becomes brighter when it is moved closer to a subject and fades as it is moved further away.

The term 'square' quantifies the amount by which intensity declines. This law is used to calculate the difference in the illumination of a subject as it is moved closer to or further from the light source. Hence its importance in photography, particularly studio portraiture (although it can also be relevant in other environments).

To provide a practical example of the concept in layman's terms: if you move a light source that was one metre from the subject to two metres away, you reduce the intensity of light falling on the subject to one quarter of the amount reaching it at one metre's distance. Similarly, if you want to halve the amount of light on the subject, increase the distance by a factor of 1.4 (the square root of 2) – which means moving the light to 1.4 metres from the subject. The reverse is also true; you can increase the strength of the light by 1.4 times by moving a light that is two metres from the subject to one metre.

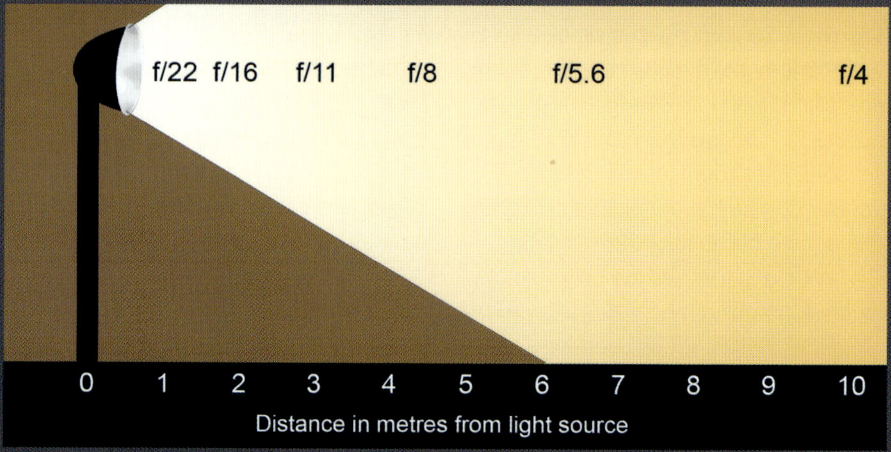

This diagram shows how the intensity of the light from any light source declines with distance. The changes are indicated in f/stops for easy reference.

Lighting equipment

In this section we outline the equipment that's readily available to photographers at all levels. Chapter 6 provides information on lighting techniques that can improve the rate of 'keeper' shots.

The main types of artificial lighting for photographers are flash and continuous light sources.

Flash: When using flash you're effectively shooting 'blind'. You can't see the effect the flash produces until after the shot is taken. This can have unfortunate consequences.

Most snapshooters have taken photos using their camera's built-in flash so they should be aware of potential problems. Subjects can end up either with their eyes closed or looking demonic because of reflections of the flash light from the blood-rich retinas at the back of their eyeballs.

While you can find 'red-eye reduction' modes in virtually all cameras, people often forget to engage them and, even when used, they often produce disappointing results. Post-capture correction can be equally unsatisfying since – as with all things – a little knowledge can be dangerous. In the hands of a competent user and with capable software, correcting red eyes in flash shots should be easy and successful.

Knowing what lighting is available and understanding how to use it in different situations can overcome these problems. Readily available flash options range from the built-in, low-power flashguns on entry and mid-level cameras through to complicated and expensive studio set-ups that are beyond the reach of amateur photographers.

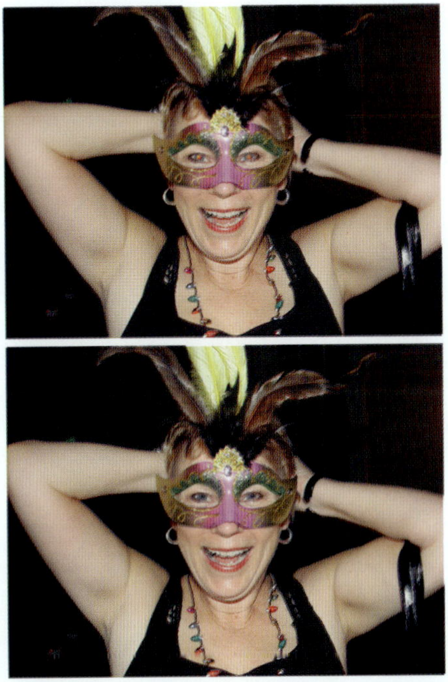

The top photo shows the way direct flash can make the subject's eyes appear red because the light is reflected directly from the retinas at the back of each eye. The lower photo shows the effects of red-eye correction, which is provided in most image editing software.

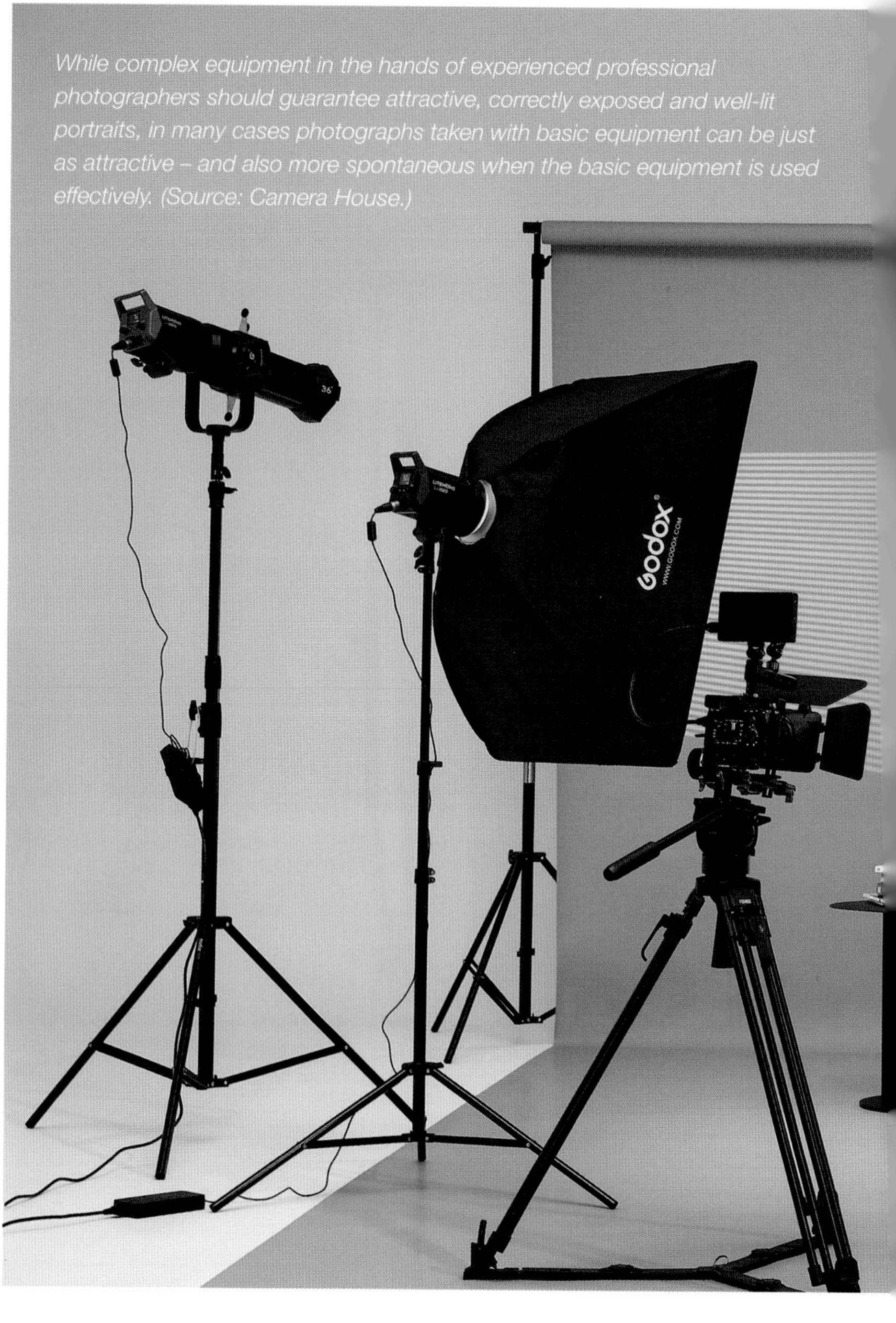

While complex equipment in the hands of experienced professional photographers should guarantee attractive, correctly exposed and well-lit portraits, in many cases photographs taken with basic equipment can be just as attractive – and also more spontaneous when the basic equipment is used effectively. (Source: Camera House.)

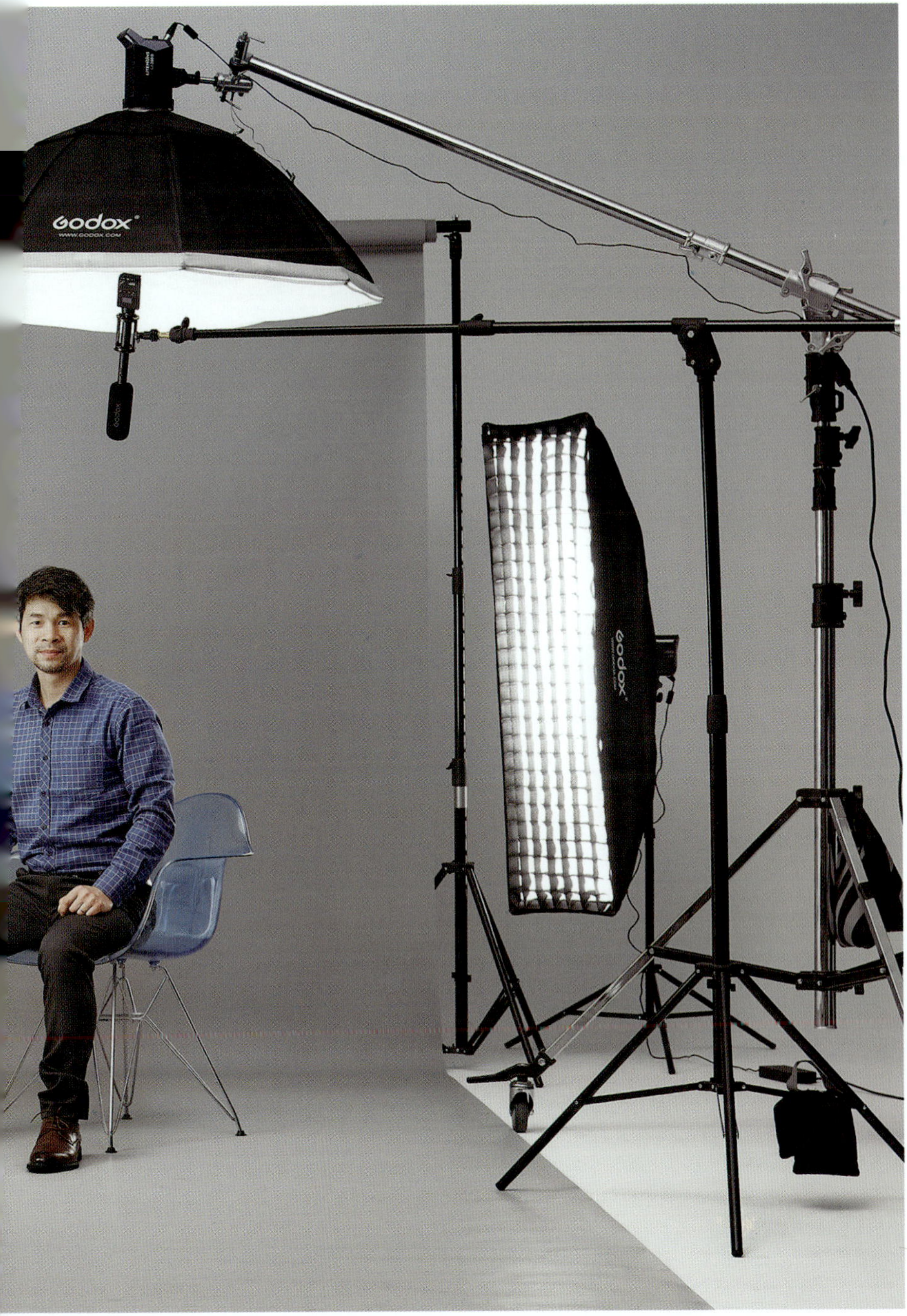
Godox
WWW.GODOX.COM
Godox

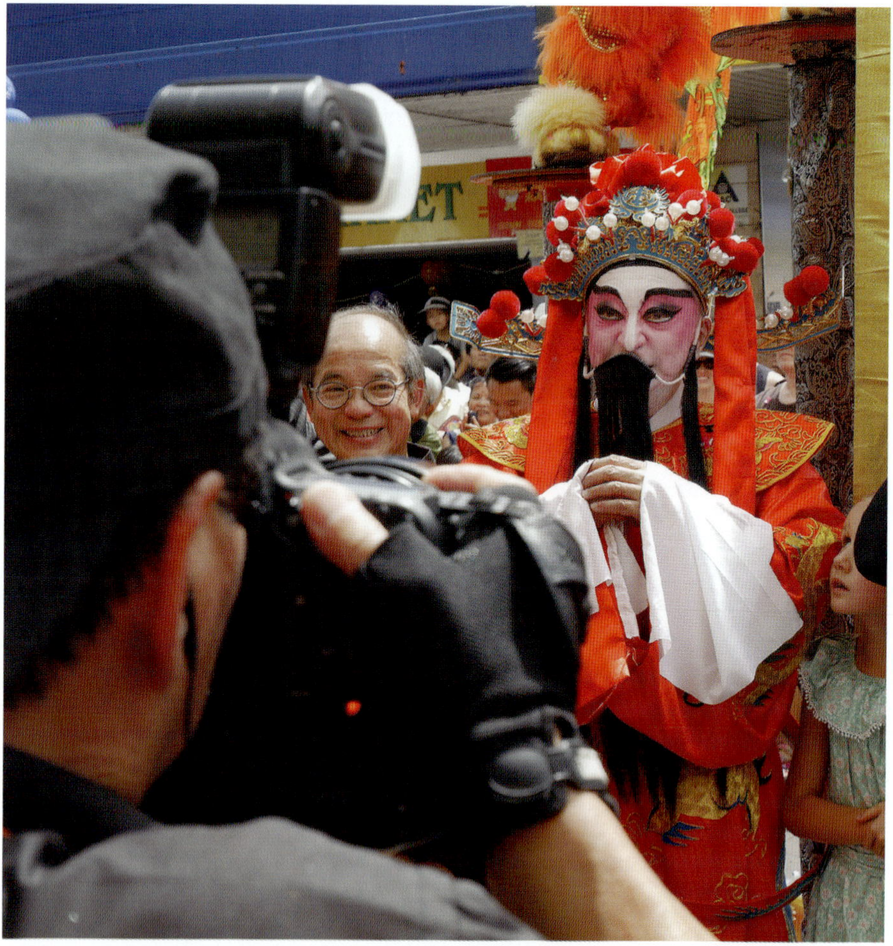

On-camera flashguns are convenient and affordable. But the light they produce can be very harsh, unless it is diffused with a clip-on translucent panel, as shown in this illustration.

Between these extremes are accessory flashguns that are more powerful than built-in flashes and much more adjustable and easier to use than studio systems. Fortunately, you can do a lot with relatively simple gear; in many situations you may not even need to use the flash at all.

The main advantage of flash is its very short exposure time which captures an instant in time. This minimises the risk of blurring, although the extreme brevity of the exposure increases the risk of the subject's eyes being shut.

When taking group portraits with flash you often find at least one person in the group has their eyes shut. You need to take a lot of shots in order to overcome this problem – and check the sequence carefully to make sure at least one of them is usable.

Interestingly, there's a scientific way to go about it. The 2006 Ig Nobel Prize for mathematics was awarded to Nic Svenson and Piers Barnes of the CSIRO, for calculating the number of photographs you must take to (almost) ensure that nobody in a group photo will have their eyes closed. You can find their original paper at **www.archive.ph/Oh9yr**.

The average number of blinks made by someone getting their photo taken is 10 per minute. Factors making people blink more than normal include nervousness, dry air, stress, tiredness, wind, contact lenses, red-eye reduction pre-flashes and social behaviours such as not telling the truth, fancying the photographer and the photographer talking about how often people blink in photos. The conclusion for calculating the number of photos to take for groups of less than 20 states: divide the number of people by three if there's good light and two if the light's bad.

Continuous light sources range from the portable and relatively inexpensive LED panels through to studio lights that can be accessorised with hoods, snoots and reflectors. They have three major advantages over flash lighting:

1. You can see the effect of the lighting immediately before taking the shot.

2. They use a lot less power, produce a lot less heat and are more comfortable for subjects.

3. They can be used for video as well as for shooting stills. (Flashguns are totally unsuitable for video.)

Either type of light source can be combined with natural lighting to 'fill in' dark shadows. In fact, this is often the best (and sometimes only) way to use an on-camera flash, as we explain in Chapter 7.

Useful links

Lenses for portraiture
www.bit.ly/38Y7bGn

Choosing a lens kit
www.bit.ly/3NFPEBE

CHAPTER 3

Candid and street portraits

While everybody knows what candid photos are – and most of us have been subjects of them in one way or another – few people fully understand the exact nature of this diverse genre and even fewer are really proficient at taking candid shots. The essence of candid shots is their un-posed nature. It has nothing to do with whether the subject knows about – or even consents to – having their photograph taken.

Candid photography lies at the heart of snap-shooting, photojournalism and street photography. It can be the most fruitful approach to photographing children, parties and family or community events.

Above all, candid shots should capture a sense of spontaneity, recording a 'decisive moment' in time. To achieve this, the photographer must master the art of making people feel so much at ease in the presence of a camera they forget it is there. It's essential to 'blend in' with the environment, whether it be domestic, official or out in a public arena.

Equipment

Keep it simple, small and light is the best advice when choosing equipment. A single camera with a standard range (24-105mm in 35mm format) lens should provide adequate scope for capturing single subjects of small groups, regardless of the situation.

Use available light since flash alerts subjects to the camera and may make them either self-conscious or hostile. Forget about tripods; as well as getting in the way, they draw attention to the camera.

Work within your equipment's capabilities. Almost all the latest cameras let you set limits to the range covered by the auto ISO function to define the lowest and highest ISO settings for a particular shoot. This is a reliable way to minimise image noise.

In the auto ISO mode, the camera's processor always sets the slowest shutter speed setting it 'thinks' you can manage when hand-holding the camera. However, this may push up ISO sensitivity to unacceptable levels by setting a faster shutter speed than you need, particularly if the camera and/or lens have built-in stabilisation.

We suggest you restrict the ISO range to 6400 or less, depending on the nature of your camera. If your camera is older than about three years and uses a cropped sensor, you may need to scale sensitivity back to ISO 3200 or even lower.

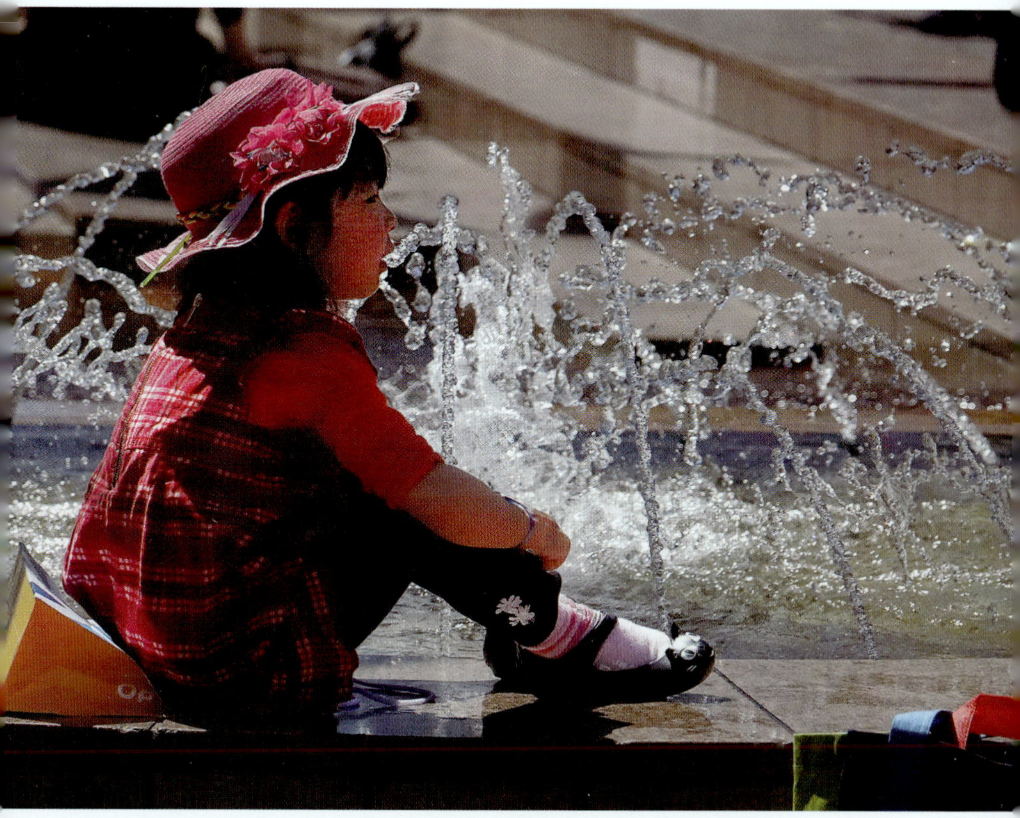

Candid photography is all about capturing spontaneous moments. In this case, using a shallow f/4 aperture with a shutter speed of 1/2000 second made the subject stand out against the splashing water from the fountain behind her.

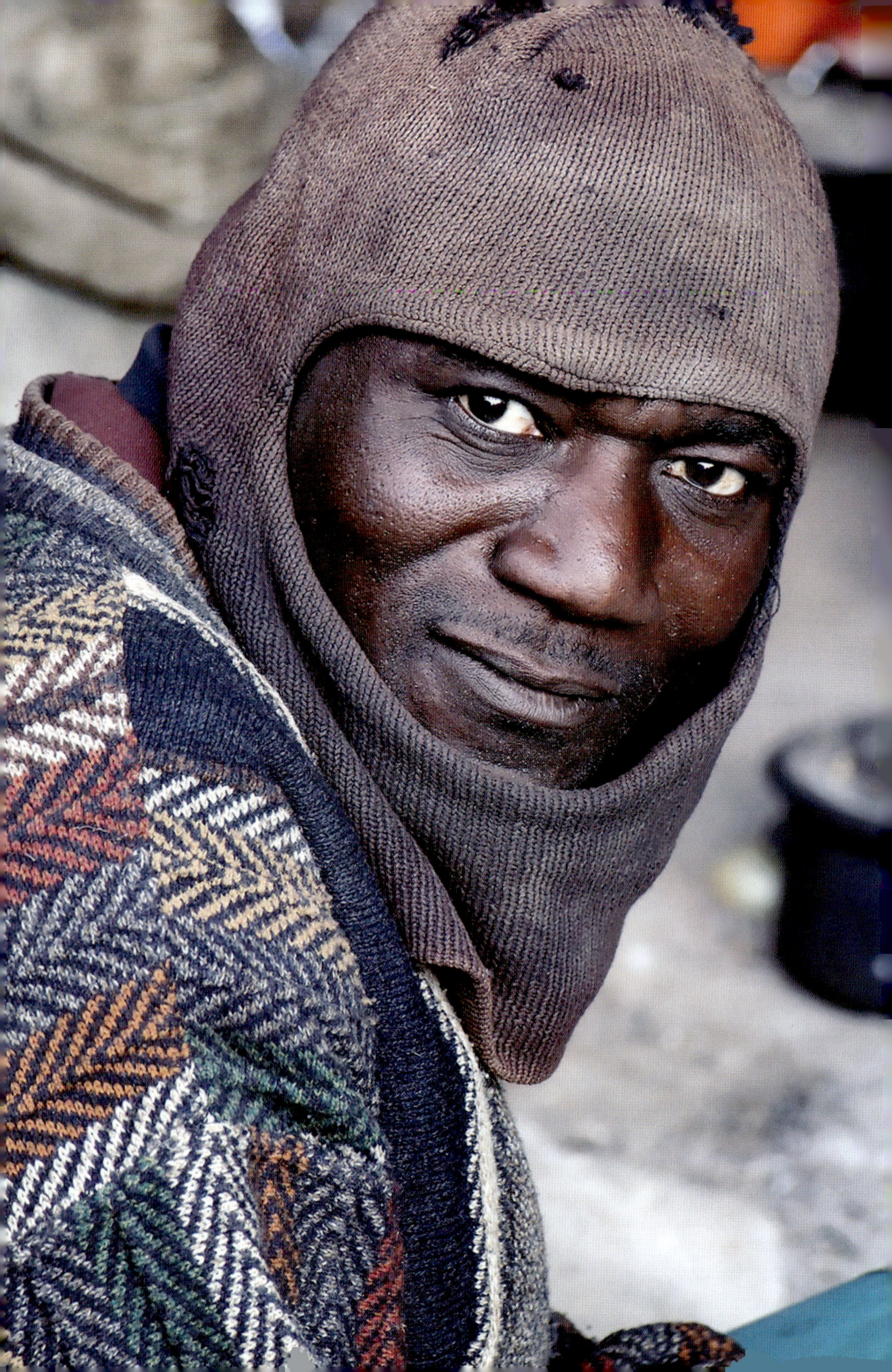

Shoot RAW+JPEG pairs to give you the best chance of getting editable pictures.

Built-in stabilisation in the camera body and/or lens provides more scope for taking photos in poor and variable lighting. The latest cameras can integrate camera and lens IS systems to provide at least five stops of camera shake correction – and 7.5 stops is not inconceivable.

Practice your shooting technique and learn the slowest shutter speeds you can tolerate in different conditions. Most cameras let you customise sensitivity and shutter speed values to match what you can handle with the lens you are using, taking account of available stabilisation.

Shooting tips

The best results are achieved by photographers who are part of the scene; close to the action but not drawing attention to themselves.

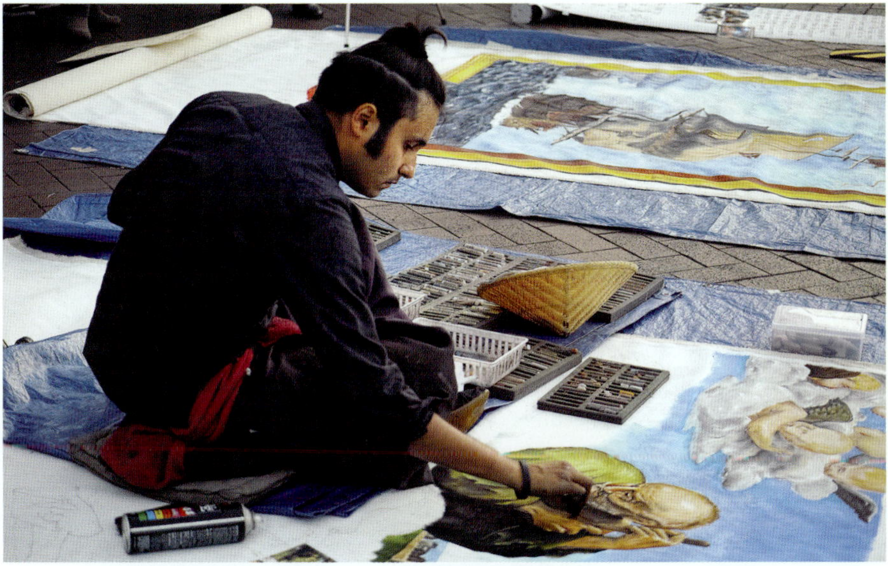

Left: Eye contact is a great way to engage with the viewer and should be attempted when shooting close-up portraits.

Above: Flash would have distracted the subject and also produced an uneven light distribution due to the inverse-square law. Shots like this are only possible with ambient lighting.

Don't attempt to hide; it only draws attention and makes people suspicious of your intentions. If you keep thinking people don't notice you you're more likely to behave in a way that keeps you 'below the radar'.

Survey the scene thoroughly before you start shooting. Look for useful vantage points, move around and have your camera ready to record the instant a 'decisive moment' crops up.

Success comes from practice and the confidence you develop as a result.

It's easier to take photos in busy places where there's plenty of action. Not only is your choice of subjects broader, you're also less likely to stand out in a crowd. Trust your instincts. If it feels right to take pictures, it probably is; don't shoot when it feels wrong or dangerous.

In potentially tricky situations, it may help to be accompanied by a friend who can provide backup support. You could also try shooting from the hip, either guessing how to frame the shot and using a wide angle lens with plans to crop the frame later to achieve the result you want or using the LCD monitor to frame the scene. High-resolution cameras (over 20-megapixels) are needed in situations that require extensive cropping.

Find a spot with a useful background or frame for your pictures and then wait for the special moments to occur. This tried-and-proven strategy can often be the best way to obtain attractive lighting and shooting angles.

Don't be afraid to ask people if you can photograph them. However, if your subject is an artist of any type and you want to photograph them with their work, don't be surprised if they refuse. It's perfectly legitimate for them to want to protect their original concepts from being replicated by others – and you should respect that.

Street performers and buskers are logical targets for your camera. Since they want to attract attention, they're used to being photographed and often 'perform' for your camera. Be generous with what you toss in their hats.

Right: Shooting with long lenses and wide aperture settings can produce some interesting results. This portrait was recorded with a compact, extended-zoom-range camera using a 500mm equivalent focal length at f/4 with ISO 6400 sensitivity. This combination blurred out both foreground and background details to create an interesting selective focus.

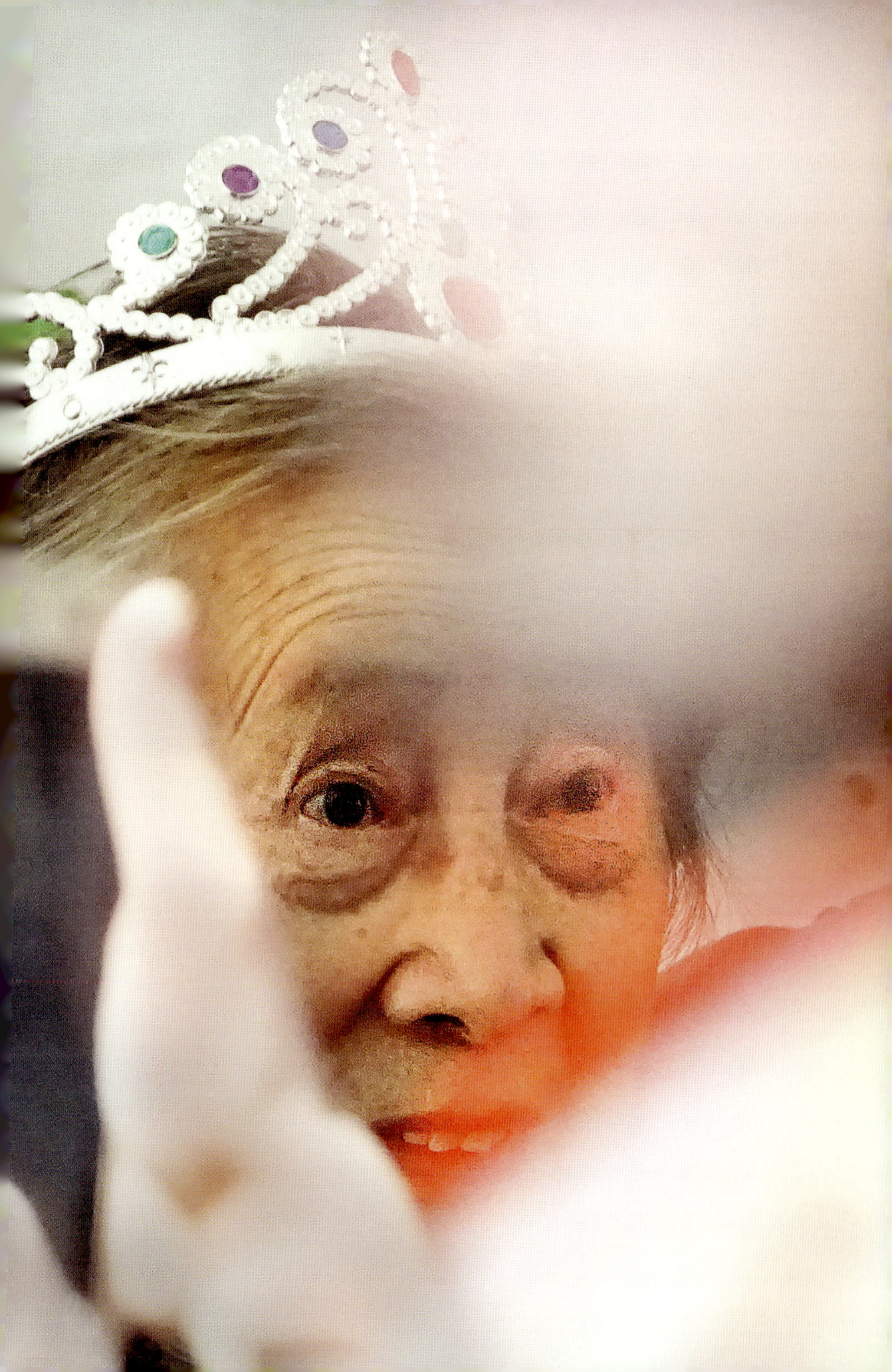

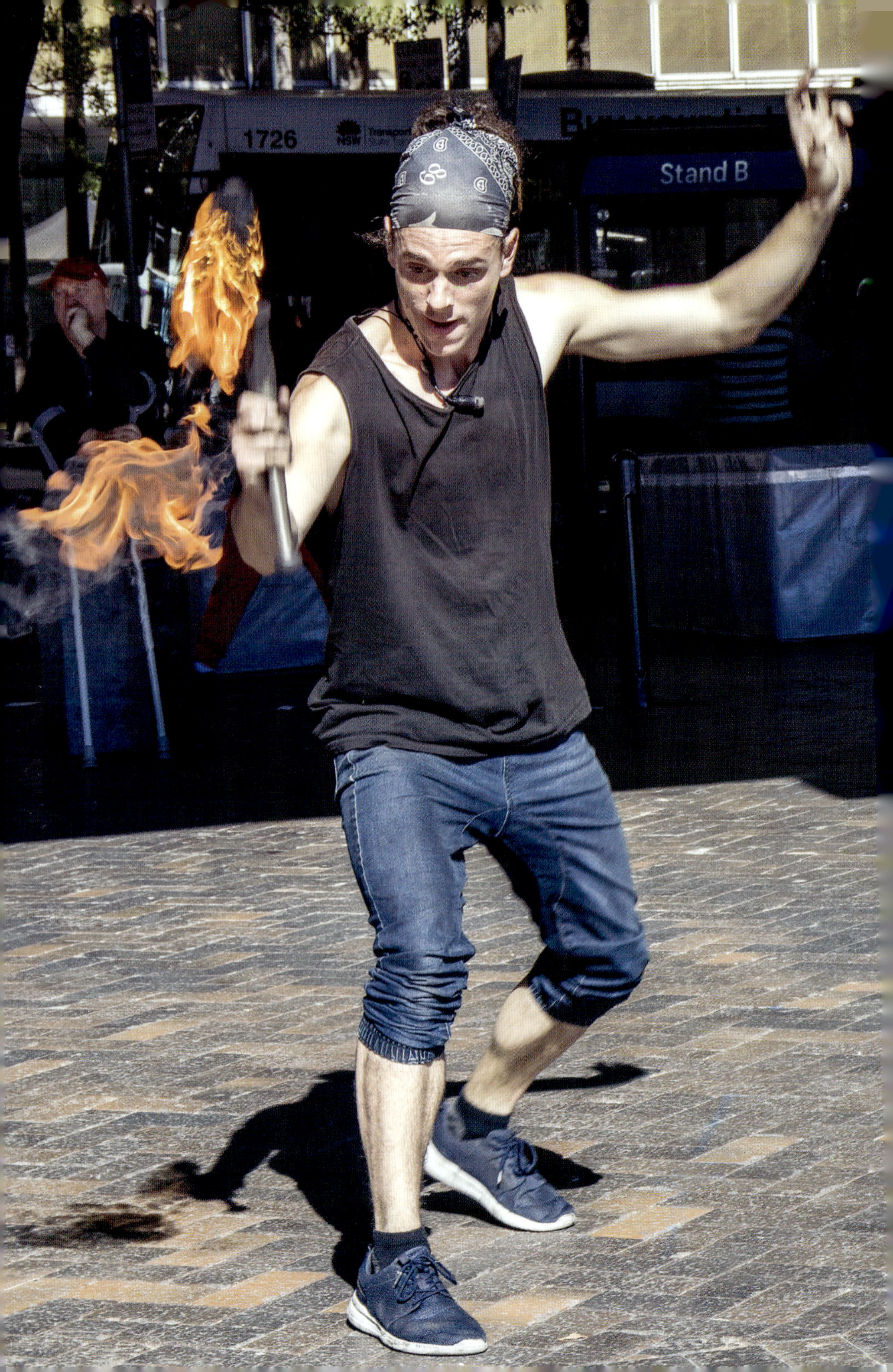
1726
NSW
Stand B

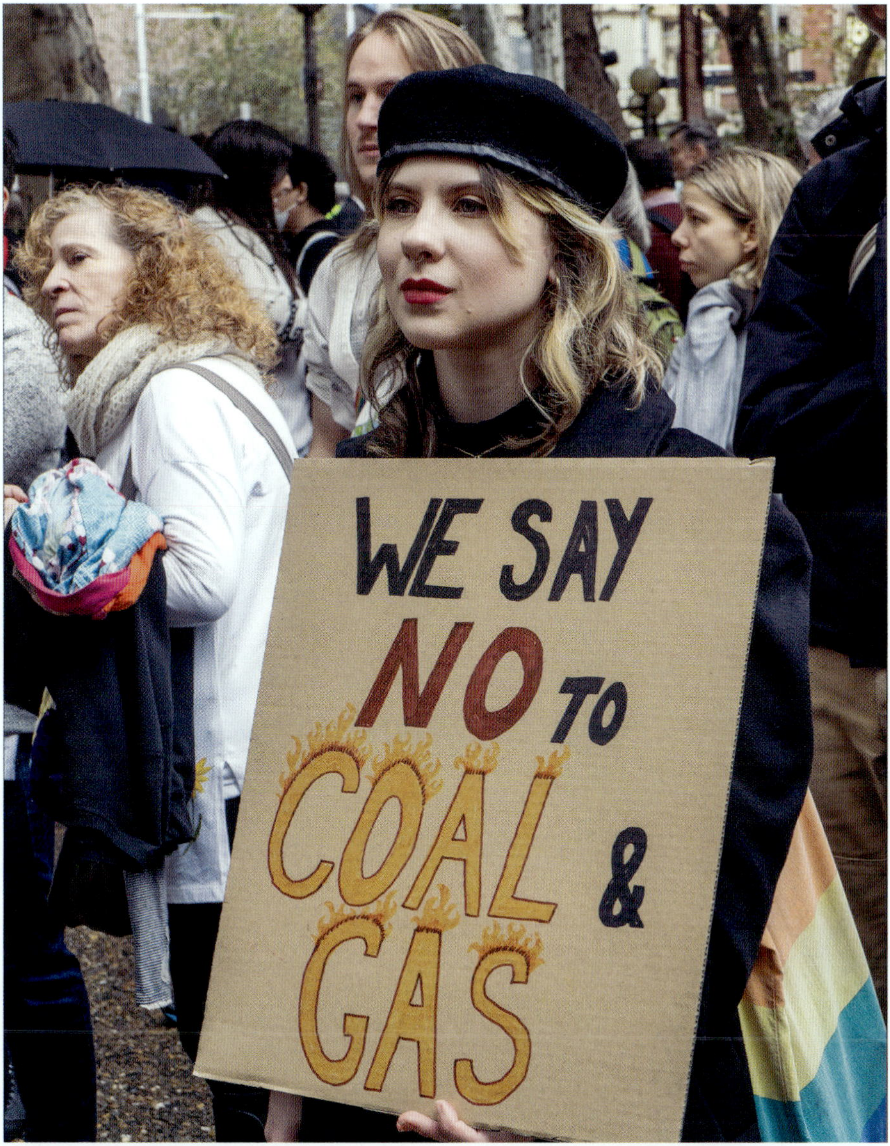

Above: Public demonstrations are a great place to practice street photography. You don't need long lenses when shooting subjects in the crowd.

Left: Pictures like this are possible if you choose the right spot, have a suitable lens and are prepared to wait. Taken with an 85mm equivalent lens and ISO 250 setting plus a fast shutter speed of 1/100 second.

Take lots of photos. Although you might think famous photographers took only one shot to capture 'the decisive moment', in fact most of them shot many frames and chose the one to print afterwards. Put your camera away as soon as you detect signs of hostility. Use your common sense and move on. If your approach is refused or you encounter antagonism, don't shoot! No photograph is worth an unpleasant argument.

Useful links

Street photography shooting tips
www.bit.ly/3LZBgDd

In the corridors of power
www.bit.ly/3N2sNjJ

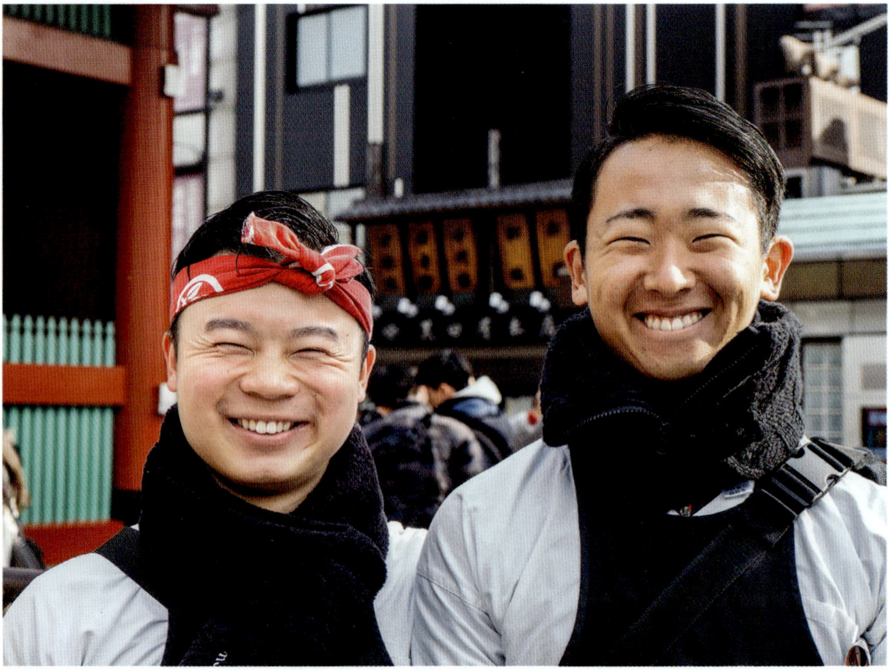

Above: Don't be afraid to ask people if you can photograph them. This pair of buskers in Tokyo actually asked for this picture to be taken!

Right: Street performers can make wonderful subjects for your camera.

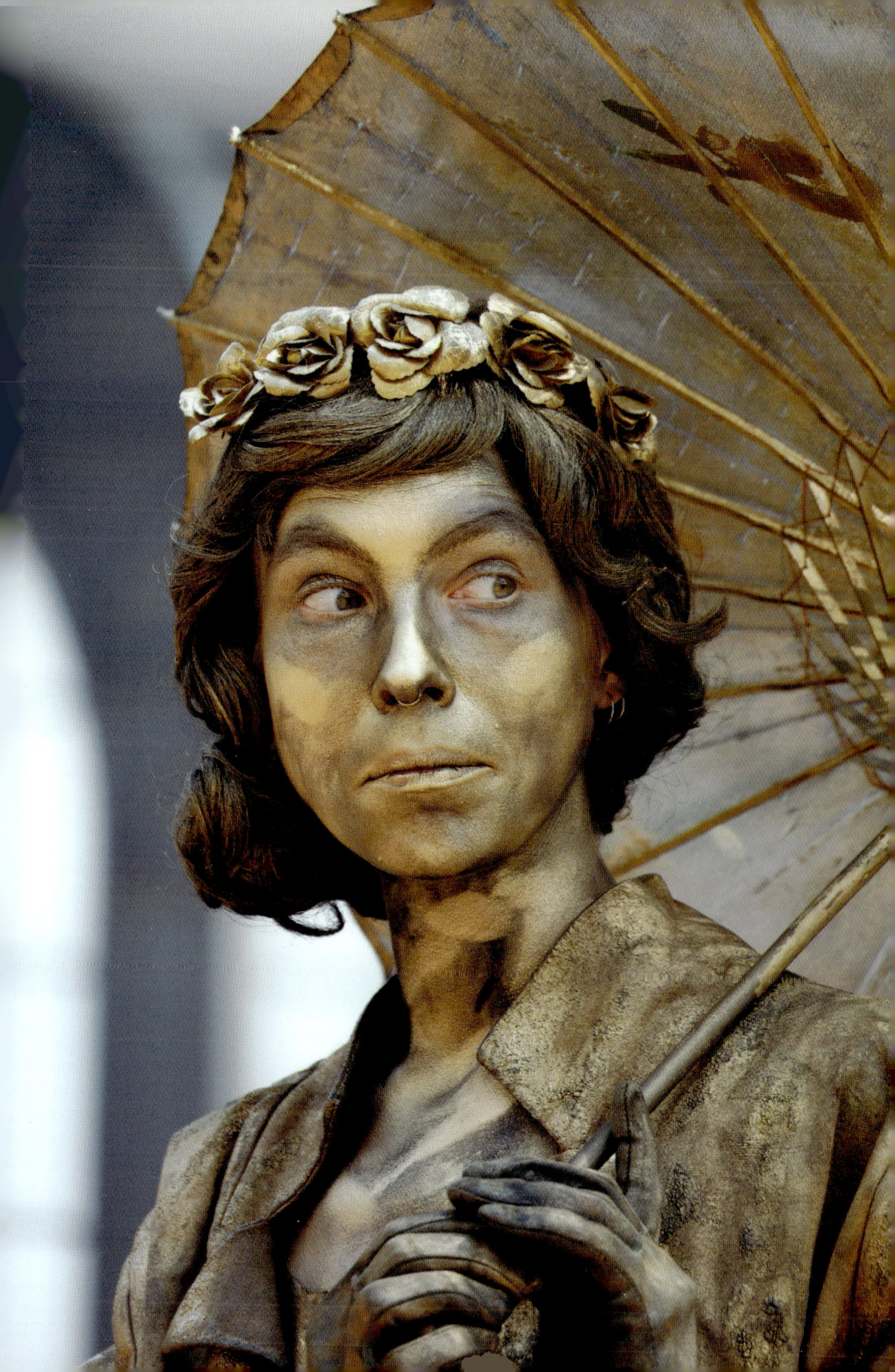

Rules and regulations

Australia has no Right to Privacy legislation that protects a person's image as such, although the Commonwealth Privacy Act of 1988 provides some protection against the collection, use and disclosure of personal information. State laws can also provide some privacy protection. However, in the main, these laws apply to personal information; not photographs.

In most places you are free to take photos of people, buildings or public places without seeking permission. This includes photographs containing people you don't know – as long as they have been taken in a public place and the photographs are for your own use. Situations where someone would 'reasonably expect to be afforded privacy' are off-limits if the subject has not given permission.

Any photographs that will be used for advertising or placing with a picture agency MUST be accompanied by a signed model release giving permission for you to sell the image. Image libraries also require model releases for any shots that contain recognisable people, even when they involve side or rear views. A sample photographer's model release form can be downloaded from the Arts Law Centre of Australia's website at **www.artslaw.com.au**.

Most states outlaw any action that could be construed as peeping or prying upon another person. Stalking people is also outlawed and photography that could be construed as child pornography can result in criminal charges.

When it comes to taking pictures on private land or in sports grounds, theatres, museums or similar public spaces, permission may be required. Shooting non-commercial pictures is normally permitted but permission is required if shots are to be sold.

Federal Government legislation makes it illegal to photograph defence installations and military bases. Your camera may be confiscated and you risk arrest if you attempt to do so. Other Government property, such as ports, railway yards, electrical installations and similar establishments, is also off-limits.

As far as privacy is concerned, situations that are covered by the 'own use' definition include photographs that will be displayed in exhibitions, published in magazines and online 'blogs' and entered in competitions – as long as no payment is made for use of the photographs. Note that some competition and exhibition organisers place restraints on the types of pictures they accept and many require model releases for shots containing recognisable individuals.

The Australian Copyright Council publishes two information sheets (G0011 and G035) covering photographers' copyright rights as well as a general guide, G11 *Photographers and copyright*. Both are available as free downloads from the Council's website.

CHAPTER 4

Working with subjects

Some people are happy to pose for the camera, while others are more hesitant and a few are really reluctant to have their picture taken thinking they're 'not photogenic'. Yet few things are more rewarding for a portrait photographer than creating a striking image of somebody who previously felt they looked horrible in photos.

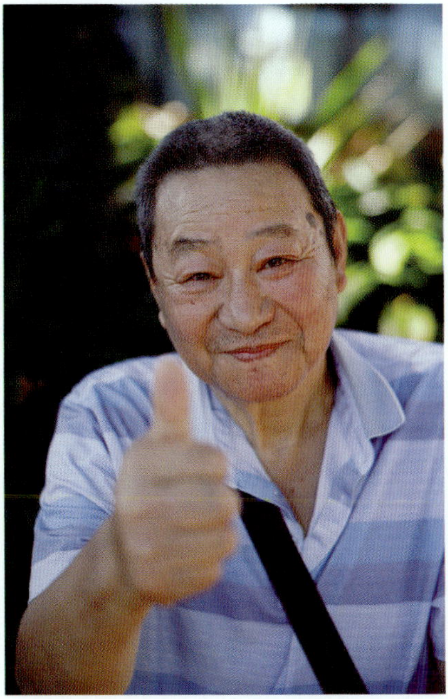

Some people are happy to pose for the camera and even ask for their picture to be taken. It's easy to highlight their personality in even a simple shot.

Few people are aware that being photogenic depends more on how someone behaves in front of the camera than their actual appearance. Relaxed and confident subjects make it easier for the photographer to find the characteristic angles, poses and lighting that will highlight the subject's personality and strengths. It is these factors that make a 'real' portrait.

In this chapter we provide some tips on building subjects' confidence and obtaining the best outcomes from a shooting session. We assume the photographer has appropriate equipment ready for the shoot, has already established a suitable location and decided on the lighting and props to be used.

The only thing left is to work with the subject with the aim of portraying the "essence" of the person.

The critical connection

An essential key to taking a good portrait is allowing the time to connect and consider the available options. Because the best portraits are obtained when there is a genuine rapport between the photographer and the subject(s), if possible, the photographer should try to learn about the subject and what their interests are before taking any shots.

Take a little time as well to think about what to include in the shot and how to compose it before pressing the shutter button. But, don't fuss around too long or the subject can become restless and the moment may be lost.

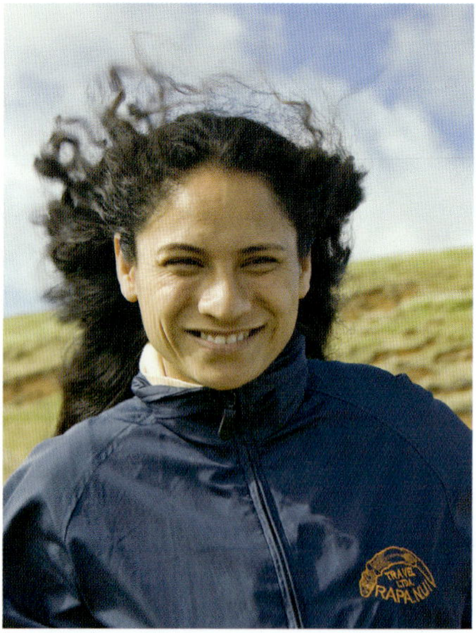

Above: Being alert to spontaneous reactions enables you to capture portraits that say a lot about the subject.

Right: Establishing rapport with the subject is essential for capturing a relaxed and attractive portrait.

One proven way to encourage subjects to relax is to start by taking straightforward shots with simple lighting set-ups. Don't ask for anything out of the ordinary and comment favourably after every couple of shots (even if the shots aren't quite what you've been looking for).

As you complete all the basic shots and the subject becomes more relaxed, suggest they might like to try something different. Experiment with different angles – including having the subject lying on a couch or the floor, climbing a ladder or peering around the edge of a door. You might also ask them to jump or make faces or introduce a few simple props that fit in with the scene and/or their personality.

If they still aren't relaxed, you could cover part of the subject's face with clothes or hair, or use hats or scarves to add interest to the head and complement a standard head-and-shoulders portrait. Alternatively you could focus on a specific body part, such as the subject's hands, eyes or mouth, the curl of a hand or the light in their hair; anything that could show more about the individual.

Every shooting session is different, so you need to stay alert to the subject's reactions and respond accordingly – and quickly but calmly. Effective interpersonal relations can convert a 'let's get this over with' attitude into 'let's do something cool'.

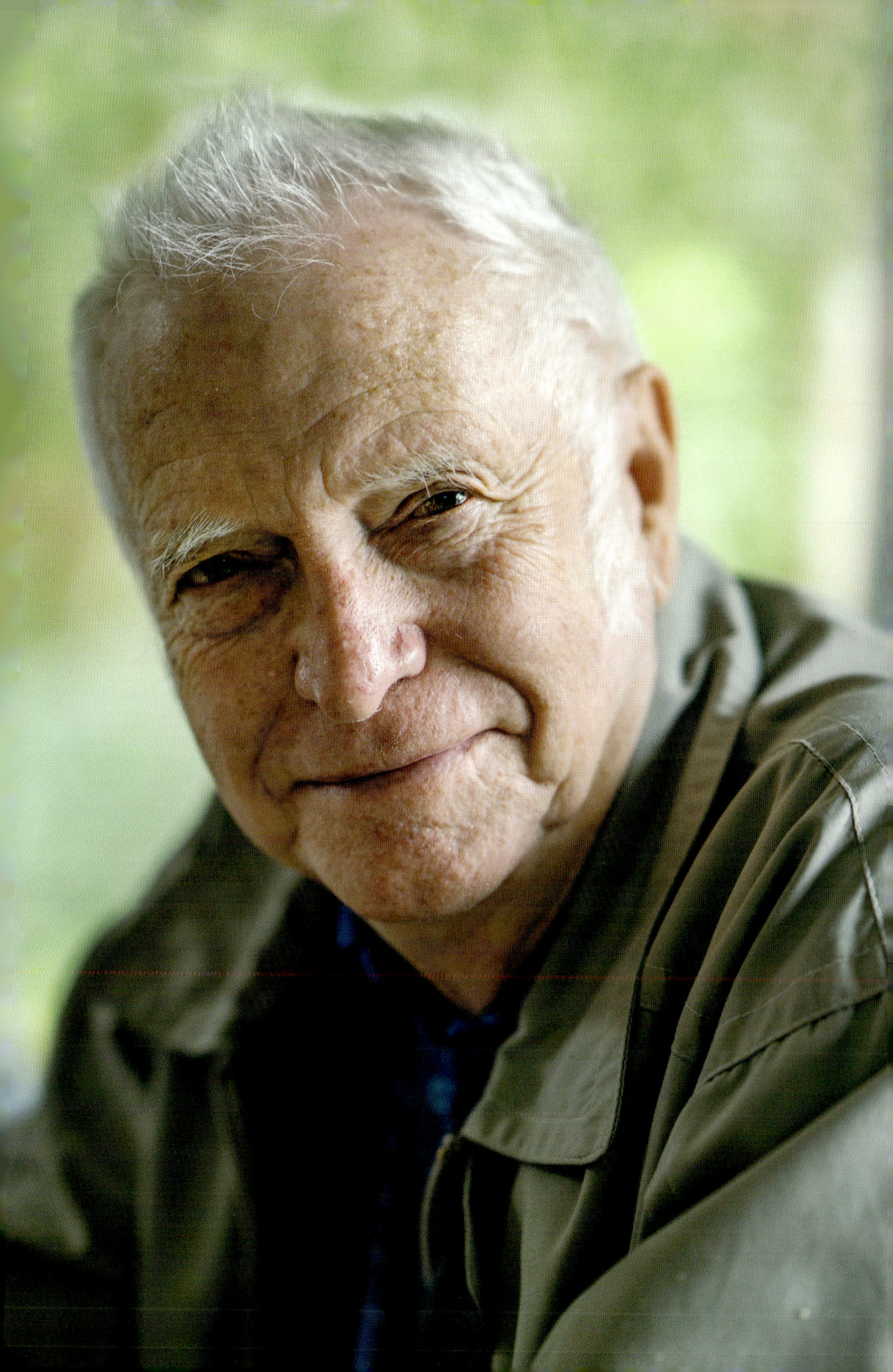

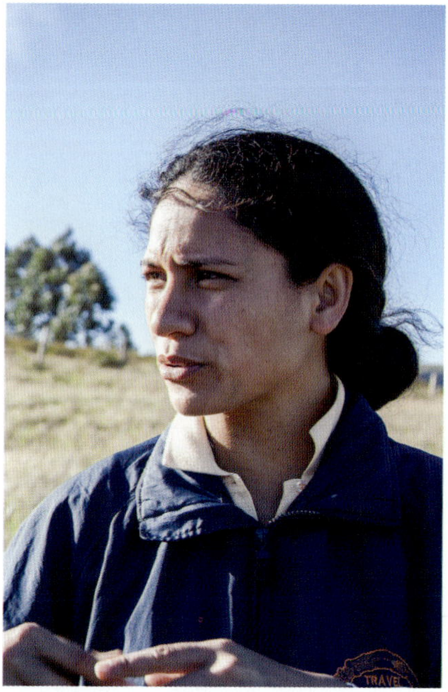

In half-profile poses, always focus upon the eye nearest the camera.

Ask subjects for suggestions and try them out if you have the time and ability to do so.

The same strategies can work with intimate, informal groups, although formal group portraits are more challenging. Photographers can usually interact but have to spread their attention throughout the group so nobody feels left out of the 'picture'.

Many elements of portrait photography rely on intuition rather than technical control. If you've set up the location and sorted out the equipment (including lighting and camera settings) in advance you have more freedom to find more creative approaches than the standard portraiture techniques.

Focus on the subject's eyes.
As the old saying goes: *the eyes are the windows to the soul*. Consequently, one of the most important tips for portrait photography is getting the subject's eyes sharp. In half-profile poses, the focus should be on the eye nearest the camera; if this eye isn't sharp the 'life' in the portrait may be lost.

Take a series of shots

Whenever you're photographing active subjects, such as athletes, people with pets or small children it can be worth using your camera's continuous shooting mode. It doesn't matter much if the maximum frame rate is only five frames per second – although these days 10 frames per second or more is not uncommon – shooting bursts can give you a better chance of recording those once-in-a-lifetime moments and expressions. It also allows you to take a series of images that can be presented together to tell a story.

For portraits of people engaged in sports or activities involving a lot of movement, such as dancing or acrobatics, recording the action as a video clip can provide you with a wealth of individual frames to choose from.

Group portraits

Group portraits (such as class photos for schools) are often commissioned, in which case the person or business who is paying for the shot sets the pre-conditions and, often, defines the location for the shot and specifies what's required. This can put some tight constraints on the options available to the photographer for interacting with subjects as well as the on-location lighting conditions and other resources available.

Arranging groups of people for a group photo is a lot like herding cats; different people have different wants, needs and attitudes and you are expected to accommodate them. Being well prepared before you bring the subjects to the shooting site helps you to minimise potential chaos. Make sure there's sufficient seating to allow at least one third of the subjects to sit down.

Be as accommodating as possible when arranging the group; logic dictates which people should be seated and

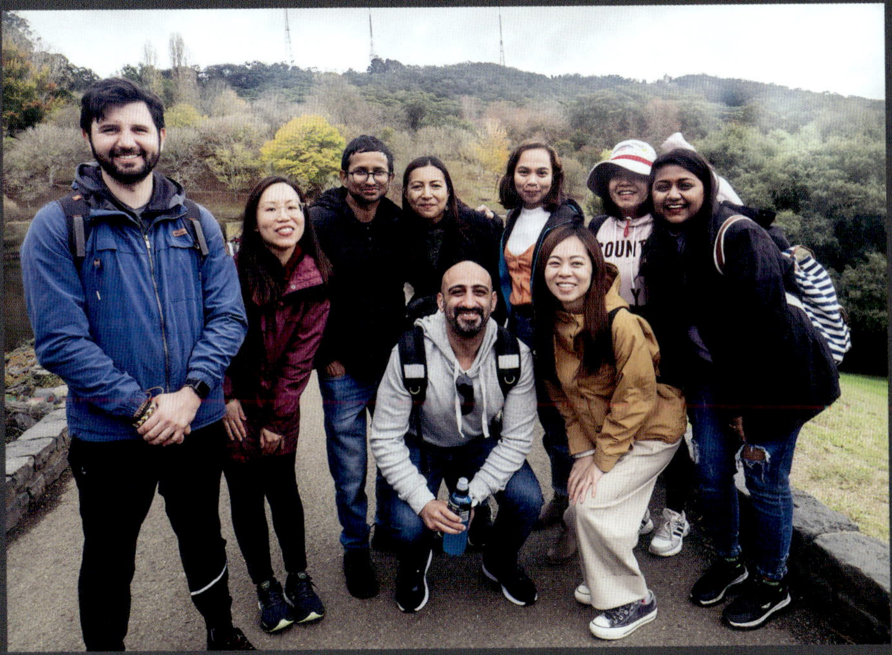

Co-operative subjects make it easier to arrange a small group for a photograph. This simplifies your job and allows you to work quickly in inclement weather.

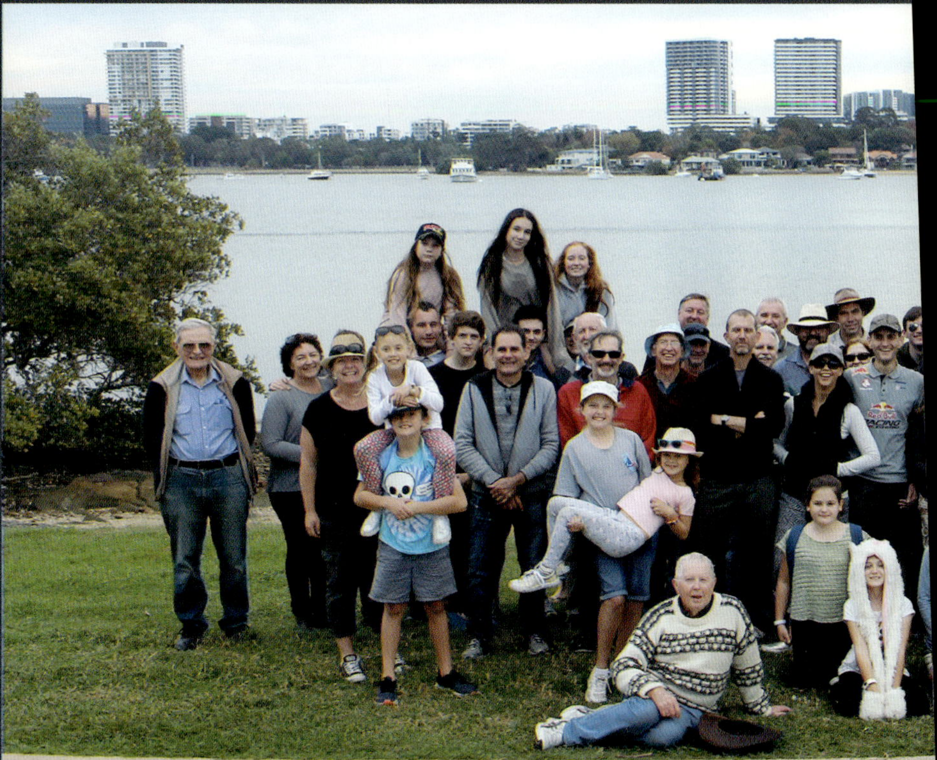

who should stand behind them. Some people are happy to sit in the front row, while others may want to hide; one person may want to be next to a particular individual, while another may prefer to be as far away from somebody in the group as possible.

When there are children in the group, they're usually asked to sit on the floor in front of the seated adults. Toddlers and babies should be held on adults' laps.

Once everybody is positioned, act quickly. If you dither, your subjects can become bored and restless. They may begin talking and stop paying attention to you and your chances of getting a shot in which everyone is looking at the camera are reduced.

Be specific when giving commands or asking anything of your subjects. Take a sequence of at least six shots using the single-shot mode. (Burst shooting can be too fast to ensure sufficient

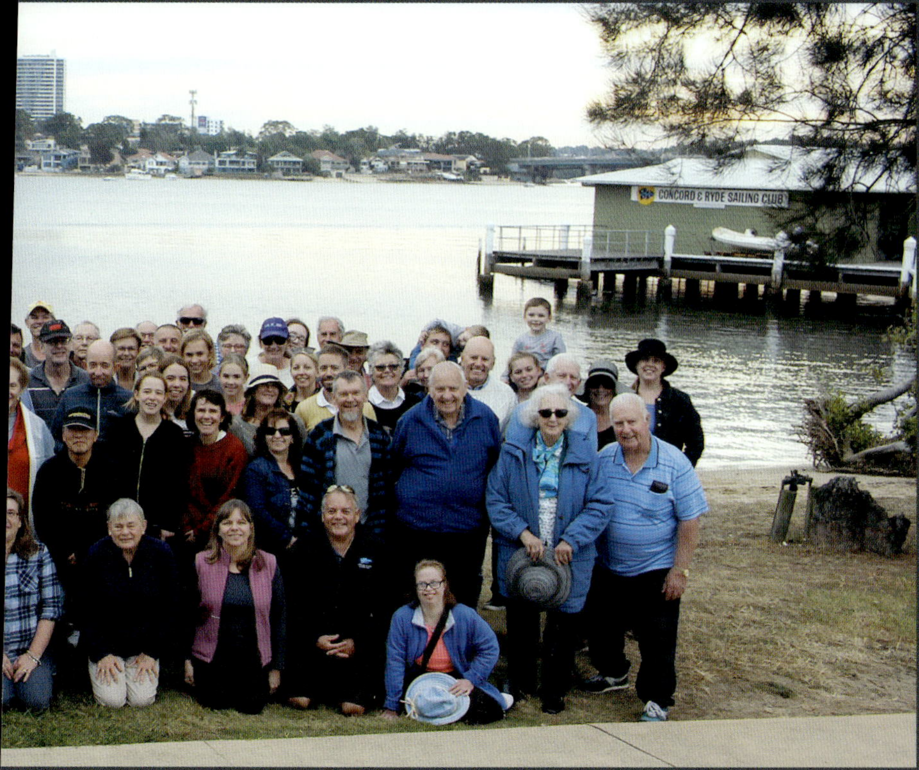

differences between shots.)
Check your shots and then adjust your shooting position (if needed) and shoot another sequence.

Arranging a large group of people takes skill and determination since individuals can have their own ideas of how they should be posed. This photograph of a

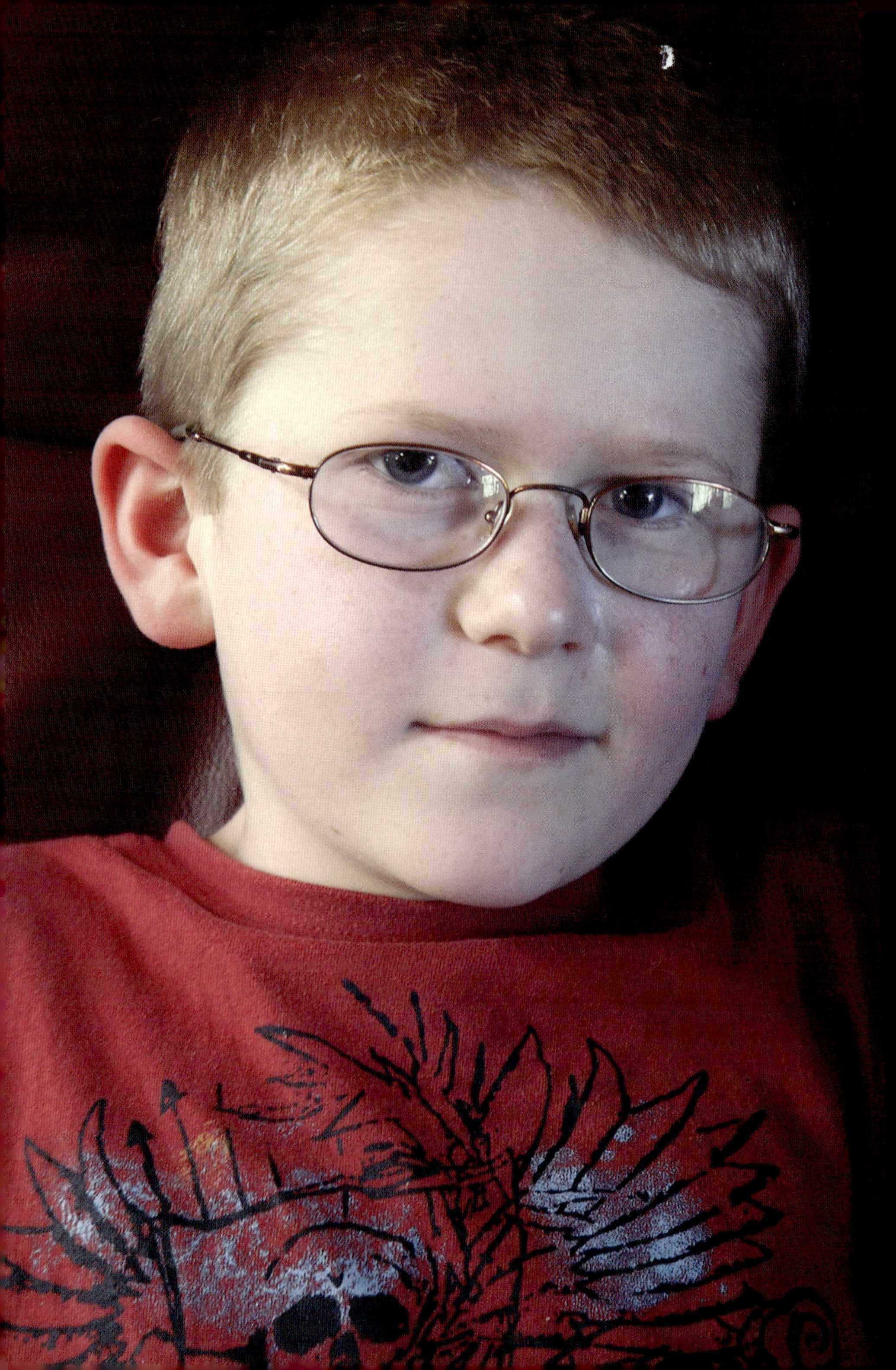

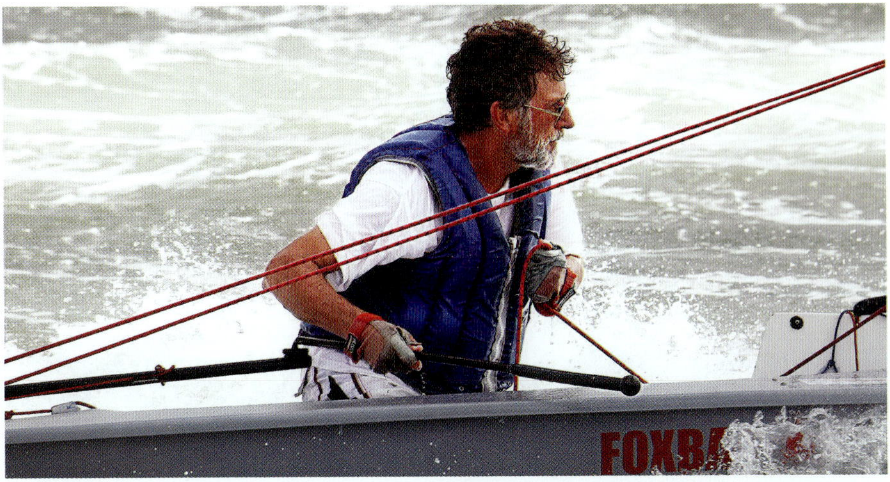

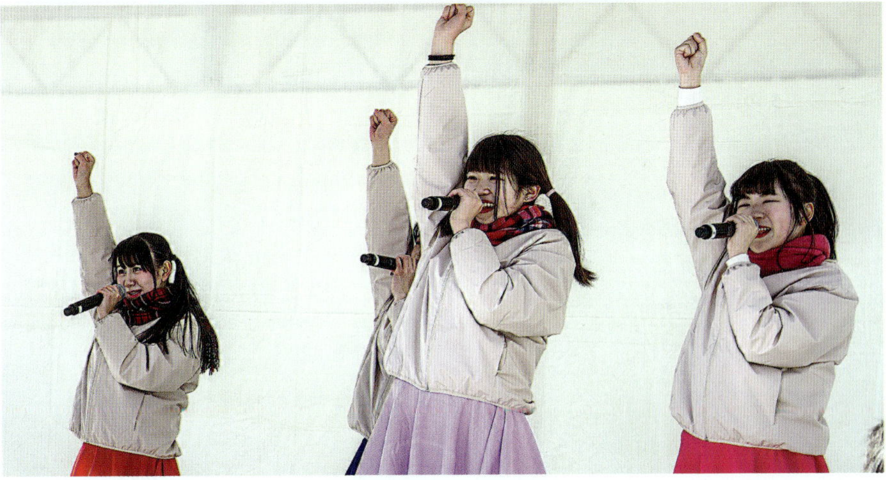

Above: Individual frames from 4K (or higher resolution) video clips recorded at 25 or 50 frames/second enable you to take portraits of sport and stage performance participants with enough resolution to produce poster-sized prints.

Left: The soft lighting in this portrait resulted from light streaming in through a window to the subject's right being reflected off white curtains on his left. Note the 'rule of thirds' composition that places the eyes roughly on an imaginary line running across the frame one third of the way down from the top.

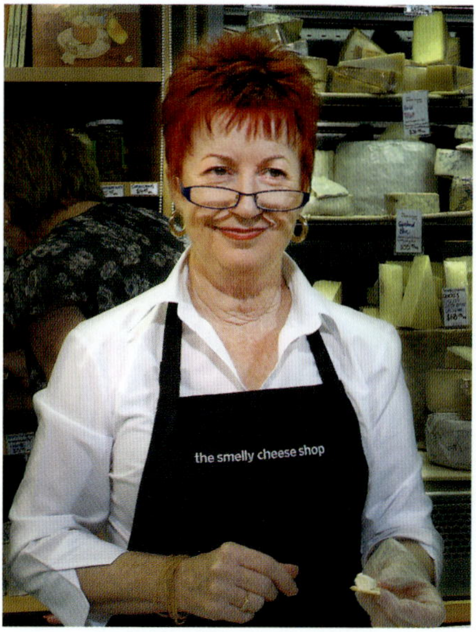

Above: Even with un-posed portraits, framing the subject to create a roughly triangular composition with the eyes roughly one third of the distance from the top of the frame and the subject's eyes looking across a wider space are natural strategies for most portrait photographers.

Right: Backlighting works well for this casual 'environmental' portrait of a young woman on her pony. The subject's face, which was in shadow, was lightened by dodging when the image was edited.

Even most smartphones include 4K video capabilities and many high-end interchangeable-lens cameras are capable of recording at 8K with 7680 x 4320 pixels (33 megapixels equivalent).

Provided your camera offers fast enough frame rates, continuous shooting is often the best way to capture subjects in motion. However, it's important to understand your camera's capabilities and know which focus mode to set to avoid disappointment due to shots that have missed the mark by milliseconds.

If your camera can record 4K or higher video, it's worth remembering you can grab individual frames from video footage for printing at up to A3 size (420 x 297 mm). This is large enough for framing. Video clips recorded at 25 or 30 frames per second (fps) offer faster frame rates than most enthusiast-level cameras – and if the camera supports frame rates of 50 or 60 fps, the chances of missing fleeting moments are further reduced.

Experiment with lighting

Soft light generally produces the most flattering portraits. You can find it outdoors on overcast days or create it by diffusing artificial lighting. 'Bouncing' the light from a flashgun or LED source off a large white wall or a white sheet draped over a tall cupboard or bookcase can produce attractive results.

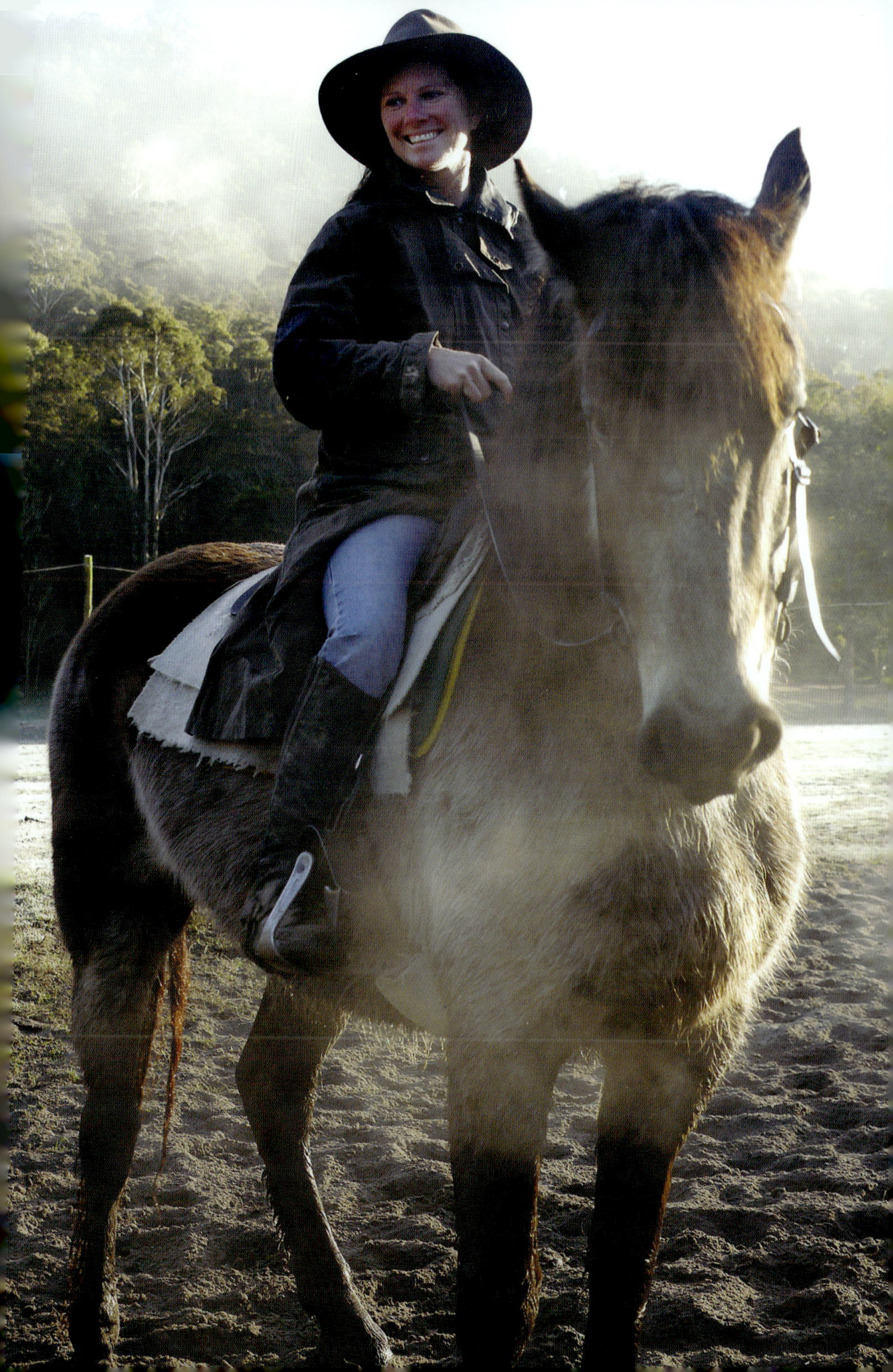

For a more subtle side-lit portrait, try using a reflector made from a sheet of white cardboard or introduce a fill light on the other side of your subject, placing it a little further away from the main light source. White curtains can often replace a reflector in shots taken with window light.

Wherever possible avoid lighting subjects from the front as it results in very flat, bland portraits. A better option is to move the light so it sits at a 45-degree angle to the subject's face. Try rim lighting (outlined in Chapter 5) or backlighting to capture subtle silhouettes.

Compositional guidelines

When posing subjects it's worth knowing the tried-and-proven rule followed by portrait photographers through the ages. They include the following:

1. The rule of thirds is based upon a 3x3 grid and positions the subject a third of the way into the frame. Normally, the subject's eyes line up along the top-third gridline of your image at the intersection of one of the vertical grid lines, depending on which direction the subject is looking.

2. The rule of space suggests positioning the subject looking towards empty space along the more distant frame edge, rather than away from it. When subjects are looking across the frame there should always be a little more space in the direction they are looking.

3. Triangular composition is just as it says, with subjects in the frame positioned to form a triangle. It need not necessarily be an equilateral triangle; any three-sided shape will suffice. Three subjects can be arranged with their heads at points of a triangle, or a single subject can be posed so the subject's head and the shoulders or arms for a triangular shape.

Useful links

Better available-light portraits
www.bit.ly/3NHw7Rf

Doing business down Art Street
www.bit.ly/3NLM35g

CHAPTER 5

Lighting, focus and exposure

Taking a great portrait is a lot more complicated than many people think. You have to control not only the scene and the subject(s), but also the lighting and the camera settings you use. In this chapter we look at some basic tips and techniques for avoiding common errors so you end up with photographs you're happy to share and keep.

When shooting a portrait, you are effectively translating a three-dimensional face into a flat plane of space. Positioning the camera in a way that complements the subject's features and using appropriate camera and lens settings play key roles in the success of the resulting image.

Human faces are infinitely variable with respect to age, gender and ethnic origins. Translating features like heavy brows, wrinkles and creases, pronounced noses and double chins into a pleasing portrait can be challenging.

1. When setting up, keep everything as simple as possible. Your aim should be to concentrate on the subject; everything else should either compliment them, or be effectively unnoticeable to the viewer's eye.

Will you shoot a natural-light portrait or should you plan for artificial lighting? When working indoors ask yourself whether there are clean walls or simple drapery you can use for a backdrop, or will you need to stage-manage the space. Can you produce an 'environmental' portrait of the subject(s) within the available space?

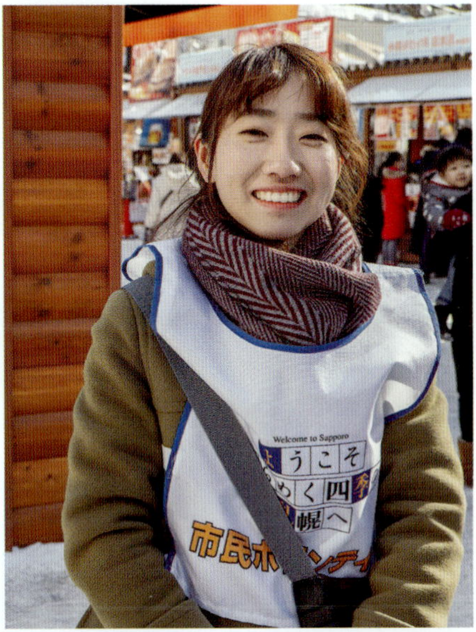

This portrait was taken during the Ice Festival in Hokkaido, Japan, where light reflected from the snowy footpaths filled-in and softened shadows that would otherwise be much harsher with more contrasty lighting.

Look for soft, even lighting and subtle tones in backgrounds that don't draw viewers' eyes away from the subject(s). Make sure horizon lines don't run through people's heads.

A common mistake made by snapshooters is shooting from too great a distance. This leaves a lot of space around the subject and creates confusion when the shot is viewed. Often the subject is too small to have any impact and viewers wonder what the photo is about. Move in close and fill the frame with the subject(s) wherever possible, leaving only enough space around them to imply they are relaxed.

2. Think carefully about how the camera is positioned with respect to the subject. If you want to make a long nose appear less prominent, a longer lens tends to compress perspective, making the nose shorter and less pronounced and the face seem fuller. Shadows and creases around deeply recessed eyes can be suppressed by introducing a front-facing reflector or using fill-in flash at reduced output power.

Double chins won't be as visible if the shot is taken from a little above eye level, particularly if the subject's neck is in shadow. Prominent ears will look smaller if they point towards the camera at an

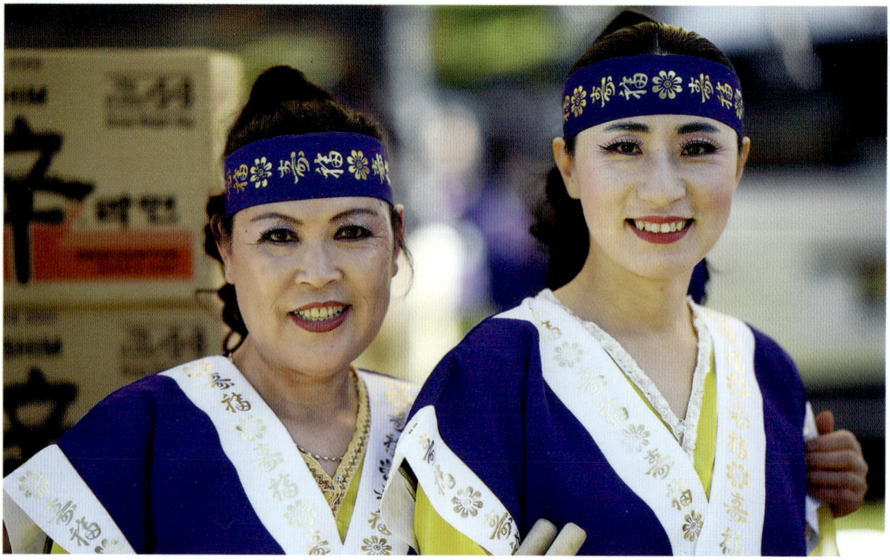

Filling the frame with the subject gives the portrait maximum impact, regardless of how many subjects are being photographed.

angle of about 45 degrees. Bald patches on heads should be shaded from light sources that can make them brighter and more prominent.

Time spent on experimenting with lighting and camera positions will be rewarded by better results. If you explain your strategies to your subjects, most will be happy to go along with you.

3. Watch out for the colour casts that can result from artificial light sources like fluorescent, incandescent and warm-toned LED lights. Cloudy days can also add a 'cold' tone to subjects' skin, especially in the late afternoon. Use the camera's white balance controls to match the ambient lighting type – or make custom measurements using the camera's sensor. (Check the camera's instruction manual for details on how to do this.)

Don't rely on the pre-sets in the white balance menu; experience has shown many of them tend to over- or under-correct. Always check exposures after you have taken them and, if in doubt, switch on white balance bracketing (if your camera supports it) or take a series of shots varying the colour balance settings.

4. If you'll be shooting outside using natural light, consider the time of day and the direction of the sun in relation to how and where you want to pose your subject. Early morning and late afternoon are the best times for a natural-light portrait, bearing in mind that the warm glow from the setting sun late in the day can introduce colour casts.

Since warm biases are mostly flattering, you may wish to keep the natural warm glow. Many of the latest cameras provide a white balance setting that enables you to do this.

It's best to avoid shooting at midday when the sunlight and shadows are at their harshest. This type of lighting is usually unflattering. Use of fill-in flash can help to even up the lighting but it will also eliminate subtle tonal transitions in subjects' faces and produce a bland, unattractive and uninteresting result.

5. When you want a natural-looking portrait in ambient lighting, posing the subject near a window where the outside light can illuminate the outwards-facing side of their face. Leaving the inner side in shadow is a popular 'split lighting' portraiture technique. Don't be afraid to use it whenever opportunities arise.

The best time to take a window light portrait is usually the early hours of the day and late hours of afternoon when light is more intense on the window. You may need to introduce a reflector (or two) to boost the light levels on the shaded side of the subjects' face(s) to preserve details in these areas, particularly when there's a wide difference in the light levels between indoors and out. White curtains may be all you need to add fill-in light to shadowed areas.

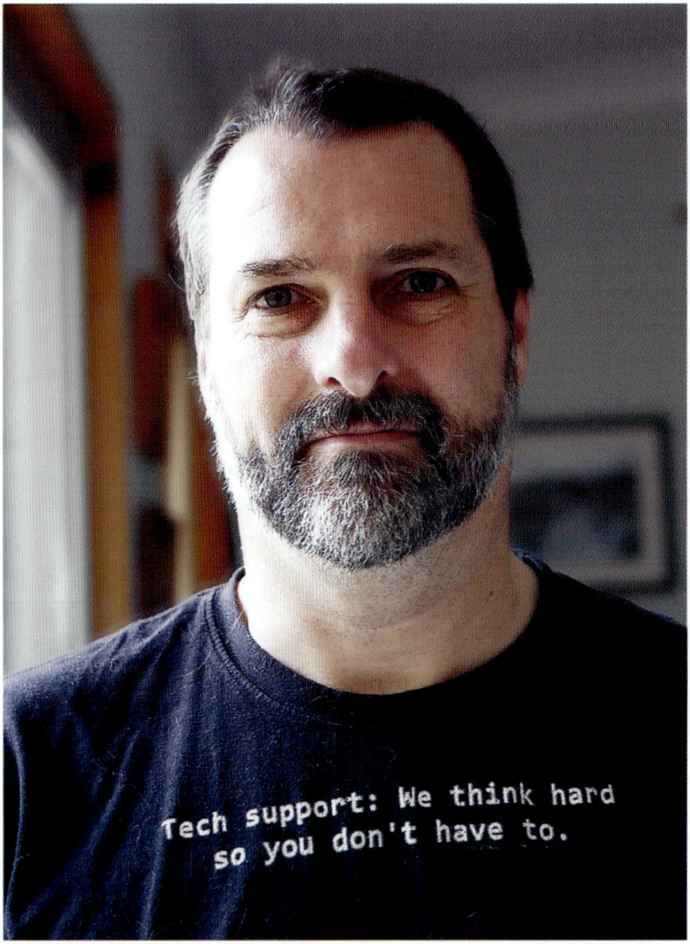

Above; Window lighting can provide a large, relatively soft light source for portraits taken with the split lighting technique.

Right: Shots taken in the late afternoon on cloudy days often show a cool cast, even on darker skin tones. The white balance control can be used to restore natural-looking warmth to the skin colour.

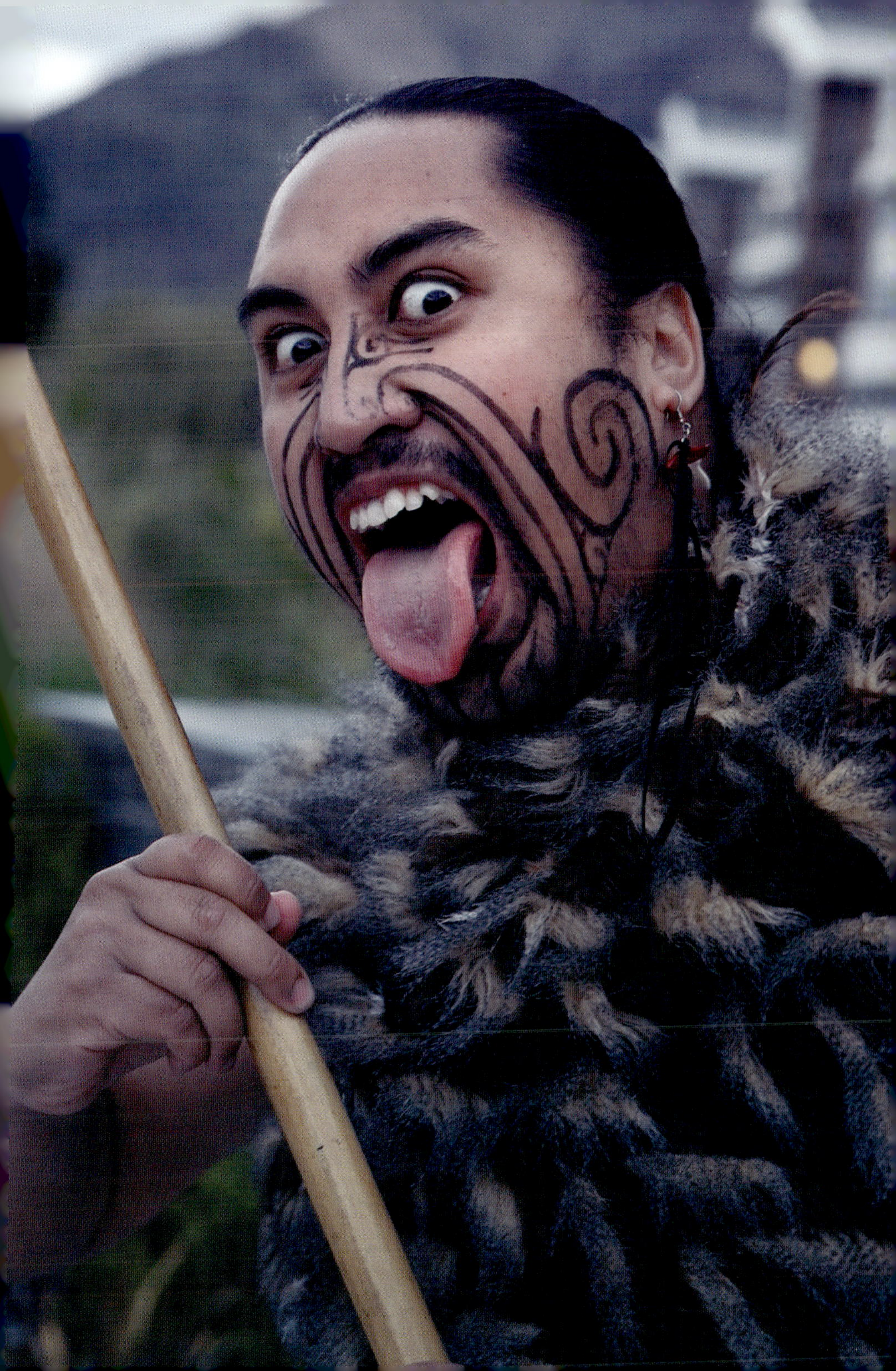

Positioning the camera slightly to the back of the subject can produce attractive profiles or semi-silhouettes. It's worth experimenting with different subject angles and reflector positions, especially if your subject is prepared to work with you.

6. Extra care is required when shooting at night because you're likely to be reliant on artificial light sources. Note that sodium street lights can introduce colour casts, as can many fluorescent lights. If you decide to use flash you will probably need to take a few test shots to see what strength of flash balance light is needed and how the flash (which is usually daylight-balanced) blends in with the ambient lighting. More information on using flash can be found in the next chapter.

7. Indoor ambient lighting often produces poor conditions for portrait shots, even though most of the light will come from above the subject and, thus, simulate a natural direction. However, it can be harsh and its direction can produce unattractive shadows. Where fill-in lighting is unavailable – or prohibited – you may need to resort to post-capture editing, as shown in the illustration on the opposite page.

8. Rim lighting involves lighting the subject, who is usually in profile or semi-profile, from behind so some light spills over onto the face and/or hair. By itself, rim lighting works best if you're looking to create dramatic, low-key portraits.

Rim lighting can also be used to add depth to a portrait that is lit from the front. In such cases the backlight should be stronger than the front lighting if it is to have any impact.

Camera settings

Focus and exposure controls are critical to success. Make sure you read your camera's operations manual so you know what adjustments are provided.

Many recent cameras include face recognition technology that prioritises human faces, even in moving subjects. Find out what your camera offers and take advantage of it whenever you can.

If you're using a camera without face recognition, stick with single-shot AF and set the focus mode to measure focus around the centre of the frame. Closing the lens aperture one or two stops down from the maximum aperture makes it easier for the camera to capture the subjects' eyes in focus, whatever AF mode you use.

Metering exposures is important, especially if there's a significant difference in brightness between the subject and the background. We recommend using spot (or for Canon cameras, partial) metering, which measures the exposure level on a small area in the frame. This works well regardless of whether the subject is against a bright or dark background and is also effective for night portraits.

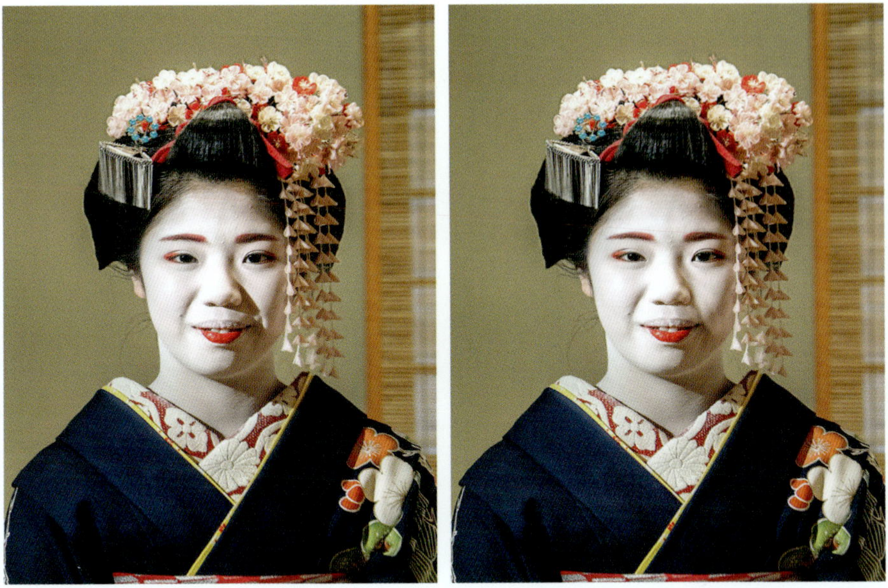

Indoor lighting over which you have little or no control can cast unattractive shadows across a subject's face, as shown in the left side picture in this pair. If you can't alter the lighting, you can cut back unattractive shadows by editing the photograph post-capture, as shown in the picture on the right.

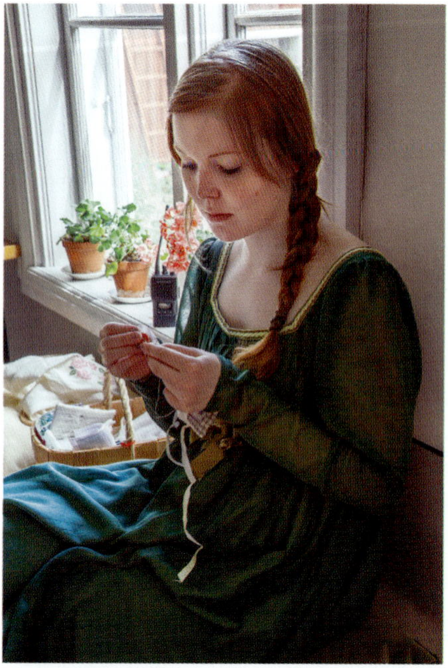

Left: Partial metering was used for this shot to obtain the best balance between the subject and the bright background. It was also recorded as a CR2.RAW (Canon proprietary format) file, which provided scope to ensure a good tonal balance.

Right: Rim lighting is also possible with natural light, especially early or late in the day. This late afternoon portrait shows angled sunlight illuminating the off-side of the subject's face, adding drama to an otherwise straight action portrait.

ISO sensitivity is very dependent on light levels although, generally it's best to use the lowest couple of settings in the camera's native (not extended) range. Most cameras, even models older than about five years, can produce noise-free images at ISO settings between 100 and 800 – and recent models often perform well at settings as high as ISO 6400. Using the auto ISO setting and defining the available range takes the hassles out of this function.

Exposure compensation may be needed when you want to produce high key or low key portraits. Over-exposure by a stop or two should provide the characteristic light-and-bright atmosphere for high-key shots, while under-exposure by the same amount can usually create the dark and moody aura needed for a low-key portrait.

Don't be afraid to experiment – and take plenty of shots, particularly when you have a co-operative and engaged subject. But don't be totally reliant on what you see on the camera monitor's screen. For starters, it's too small to make quality assessments. It may also be unable to accurately reproduce the hues and tones recorded in the image.

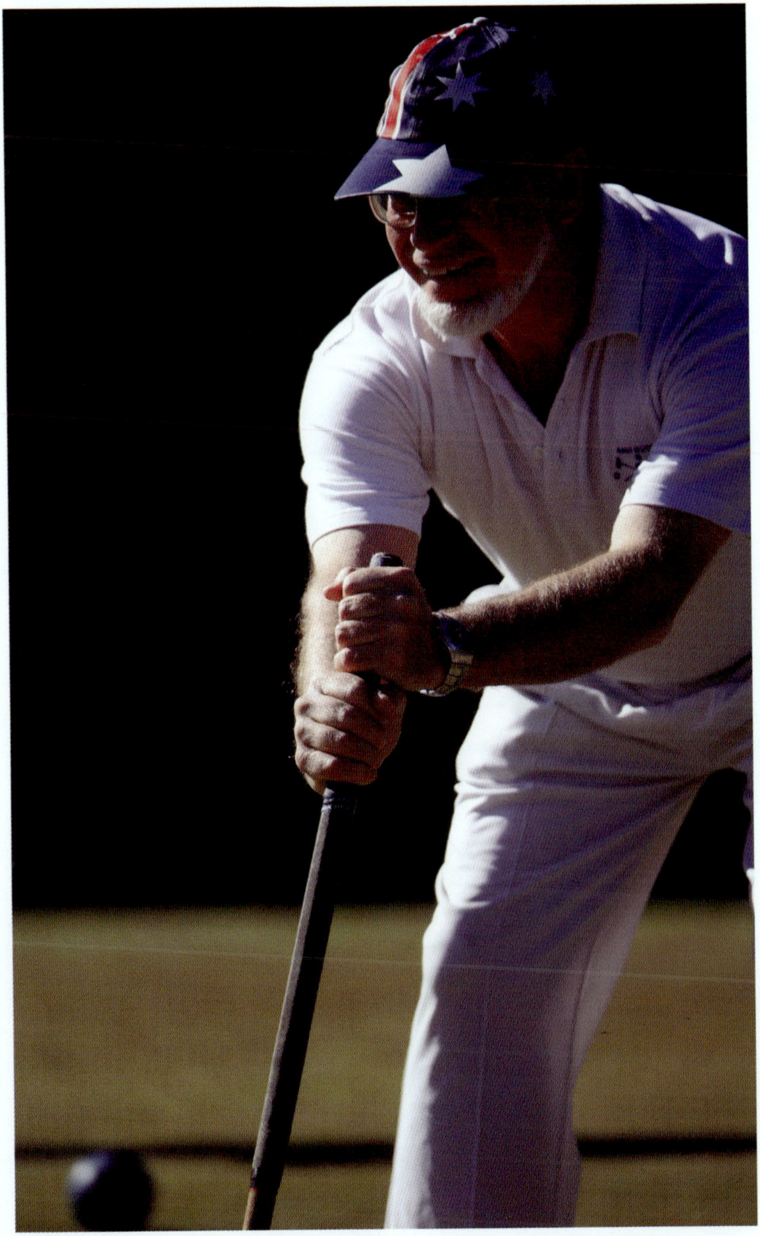

Handy reflectors

Reflectors allow you to direct light into shadowed areas to create a more even spread of illumination across subjects' faces. They provide a cheap and easy way to stop shadows becoming too deep and emphasising wrinkles and creases.

There are plenty of things you can use as a reflector, ranging from immovable objects like walls through to portable objects like mirrors and sheets of fabric or cardboard. It's important to be aware that the colour of the reflector influences the colour of the light it reflects onto the subject. The best reflectors are usually white – or very close to white in hue.

Mirrors can be used as reflectors but care is needed because they tend to be very specular and can reflect 'hot spots' of light that look unnatural. Many photographers prefer using crumpled aluminium foil, which is spread out to cover a rigid surface, like a piece of cardboard. This can work well in many situations. White curtains and sheets can also be used as reflectors, although they're not quite as easy to use as solid surfaces.

Reflectors are especially useful for bounced flash shots, which are explained in the next chapter. We'd recommend experimenting with resources that come readily to hand before purchasing specially-designed accessory reflectors, which can be purchased from professional photography suppliers in capital cities around the country.

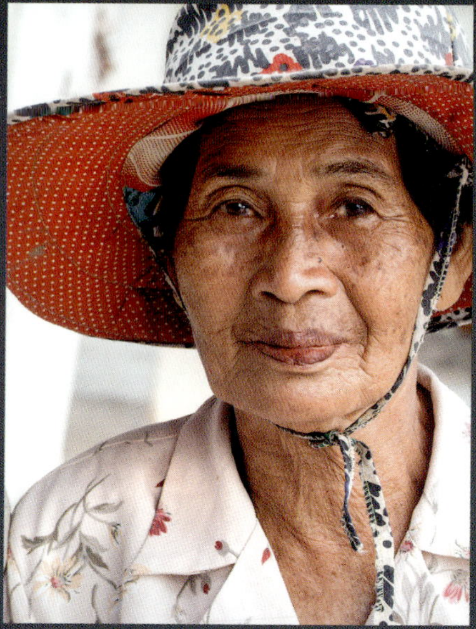

White walls in the background combine with reflected light from a cream-coloured tablecloth below the subject's face and light streaming in from the subject's left side. This directs the light around the scene and compensates for what could otherwise create deep shadows on the subject's right side and below her chin.

Useful links

Make the most of available light
www.bit.ly/3LX3Vc0

Focusing and exposure in low light levels
www.bit.ly/3wXp7tU

CHAPTER 6

Studio portraiture

Portraiture with artificial light sources is often left to professionals, although enthusiasts sometimes set up home studios and portable equipment is available for taking lights on location shoots. Professional equipment can be costly and difficult to set up, although portable kits like the one shown on this page are available in specialist stores.

There are also plenty of individual light sources in the form of flashguns and LED panels that are affordably priced and easy to carry and covered in the next chapter. You can even use a torch (or two) at a pinch.

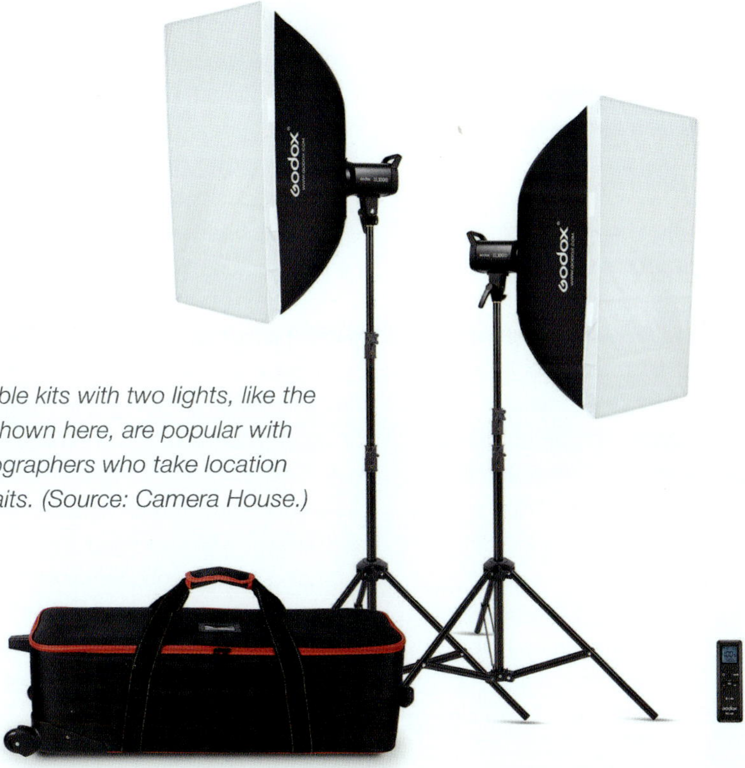

Portable kits with two lights, like the one shown here, are popular with photographers who take location portraits. (Source: Camera House.)

Knowing **how** to use light to achieve a desired look is the key to success. However, it requires more than a basic knowledge of what light sources are available. In this chapter we look at ways in which different lights can be used and outline some simple lighting techniques that can be used by everyday portraitists, based on using a single light source.

Hard and soft lighting

For any given source, the quality of the light can be classified as either 'hard' or 'soft'. Hard light creates strong shadows, which can be useful for creating drama and/or bringing out facial structure in portraits of people with formidable characters. Soft light is more flattering and is usually seen as the most desirable lighting for portraiture.

From a practical viewpoint, whether light is hard or soft depends mainly on the size of the light source and its distance from the subjects. Under most conditions, the higher the light emission, the smaller the light source and the closer it is to the subject, the harder it becomes.

Hard light creates abrupt transitions between highlights and shadows. It is common in shots taken in direct sunlight and with direct flash as well as with close, focused lights.

In contrast, soft light is characterised by large, diffuse light sources that are some distance from the subject and produce gradual tonal transitions between highlights and shadows. This type of lighting is common on cloudy days and when direct light passes through diffusers like translucent panels or fine muslin. Reflected light also tends to be on the soft side.

As a general rule, moving a light closer to a subject makes it brighter while moving it away reduces its brightness. Care is required when moving lights closer as it can create uneven light distribution. For example, the shaded side of the subject might only be 5% farther from a light source, but it could appear much darker relative to the other parts of the subject when the light source is moved up close.

You can adjust the distance between the subject and the light and the subject and the background – as well as the light and the background to control the tonal relationships between them. To separate the subject from the background, it's best to make the subject much brighter relative to their background.

Either move the light so less reaches the background or change the position of the subject so the background is several metres behind them. There's a risk of making the background too dark if they were already well-separated and you're only using a single light. However, this can be rectified by shining a second light with lower power on the background from behind the subject where it can't be seen by the camera.

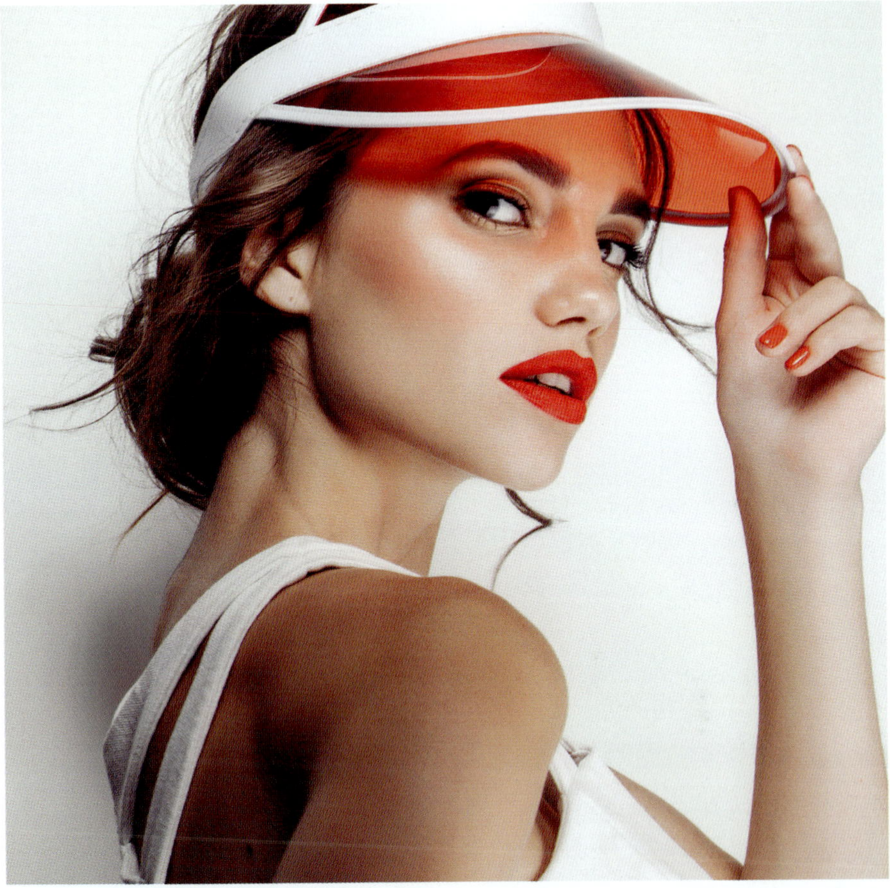

Soft lighting produced by large, diffuse light sources is generally preferred for younger subjects. (Source: Camera House.)

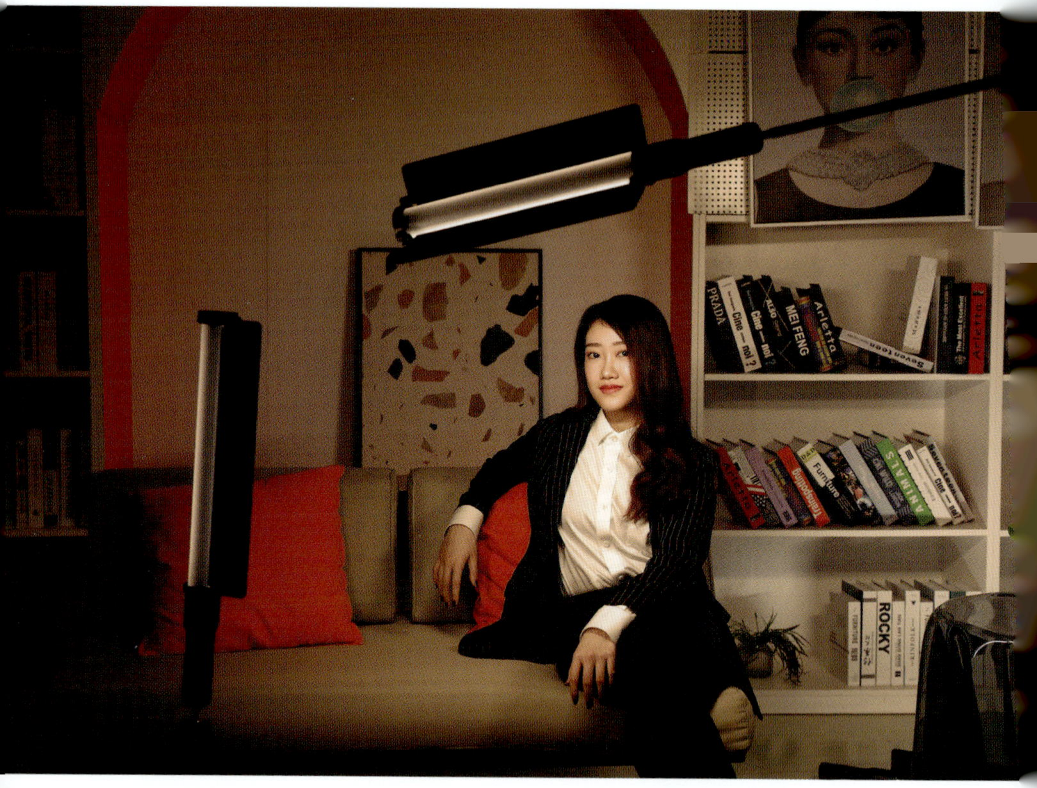

An example of the use of portable fluorescent lights reflected off light-coloured walls to create soft lighting for an indoor 'location' portrait. (Source: Camera House.)

Classical lighting patterns

While there's no right or wrong way to place lights, there are some general guidelines that usually work well in many situations. One of the fundamentals is to light subjects from above since this is what normally happens with ambient lighting. When you're outdoors, the sun lights you from above and if you move indoors, rooms are commonly lit by lights on (or hanging from) the ceiling.

Lighting subjects from above feels 'natural' since it shows them as the world sees them – although it's not without some potential problems. To match outdoor lighting the light source must be very large and diffuse; hard light produces harsh, unattractive shadows that can be unflattering and are difficult to work with.

Changing the angle of the light with respect to the subject changes how much the planes in the subject's face are lit. Placing the light source low down in front of the subject and lighting them from below casts the shadows upwards, creating an unnatural and almost sinister look.

Lighting from the side gives you the opportunity to introduce modelling since the side of the face closer to the light will appear brighter than the rest, which will be in shadow. It is up to the photographer to decide on the lighting angle and how far the light is from the subject. The light to subject distance will dictate its strength.

Some experimentation is normally required to determine which light placement works best for each subject, particularly when you need to allow for differently-shaped faces. There's no one strategy that produces a light position that is flattering for everybody – although there are some basic principles that can be used as starting points.

When you're working with only one light it is usually positioned at an angle, paying attention to how the light falls on the subject's face. The most common lighting angle is 45 degrees – from the front of the subject. The subject may be facing directly at the camera or turned to an angle (usually between 30 and 45 degrees).

Look at where the shadows and highlights are and whether they are strong enough, too strong or barely visible. Move the light away from the subject if it's too bright or bring it closer to make it brighter.

Short lighting involves illuminating the side of the subject's face away from the camera, leaving the side closer to the camera in shadow. Short lighting can be flattering to most face shapes but is often used to make round faces seem slimmer.

Broad lighting illuminates the side of the subject's face that is facing the camera. It can be used to make a narrow face look wider but is less flattering for subjects with normal and round face shapes.

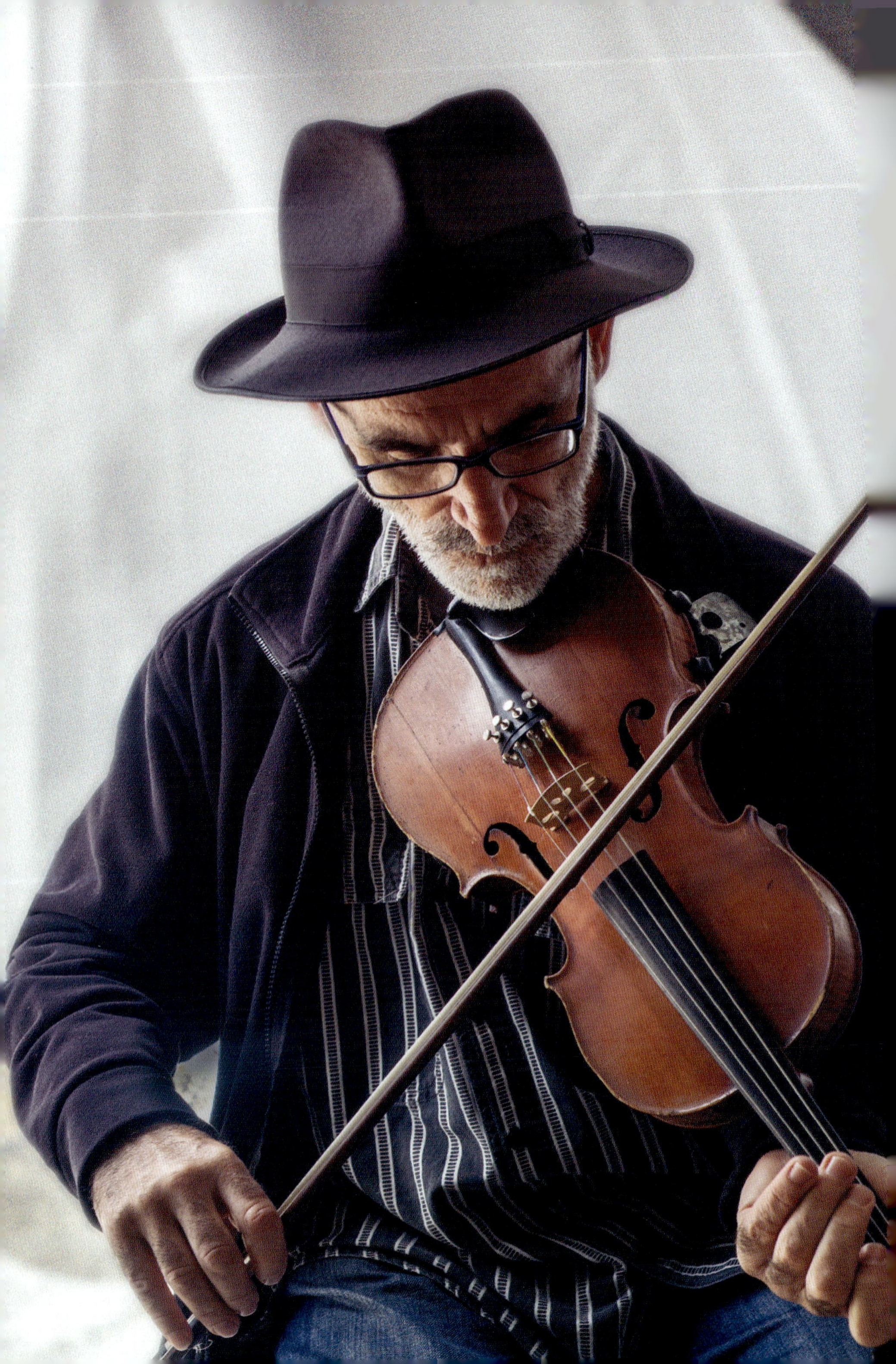

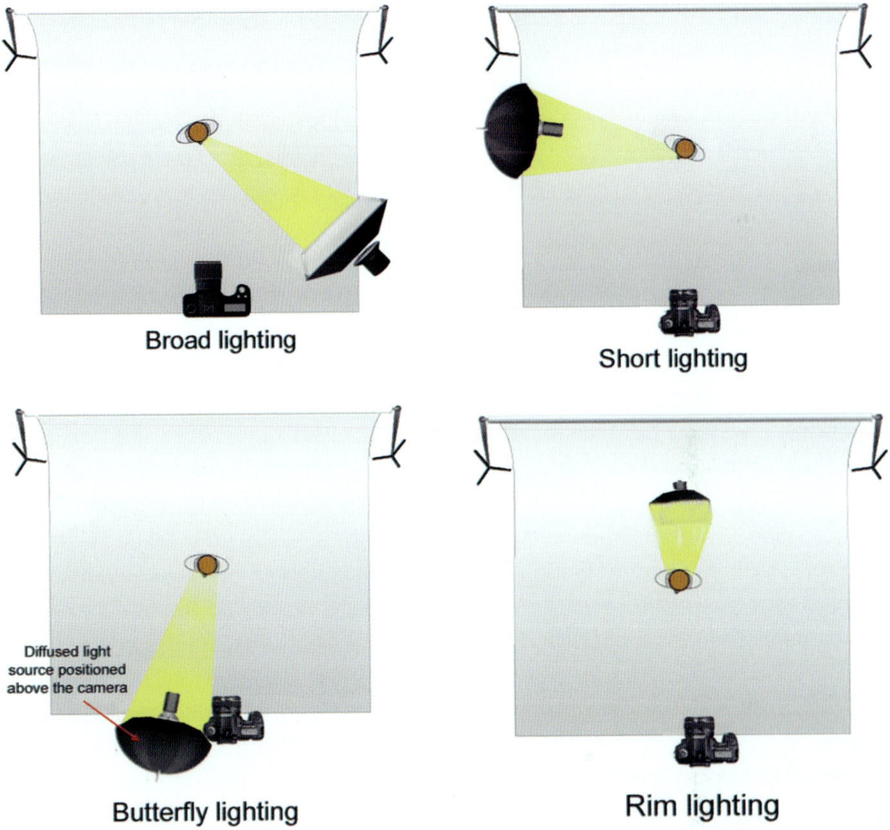

Above: This graphic shows the positions of studio lights for four popular lighting placements using a single light source: clockwise from top left: broad lighting, short lighting, rim lighting and butterfly lighting. Most studio portraits use several of these lights to provide a more natural-looking portrait.

Left: Lighting the subject from the side brings out facial modelling, which is particularly effective for older subjects. The light has been placed level with the subject's face to avoid excessive shading from his hat.

Rim lighting involves positioning the light source low down behind the subject so some light spills over onto the hair. Such rim lights are often called 'hair lights' since they are commonly used as a supplementary light to highlight the subject's hair and separate the subject from the background.

Rim lights can also be used to highlight the profile of a subject when they are facing away at right angles to the camera or when they're in semi-profile. In both situations, care must be taken to ensure the actual light source isn't included in the frame.

A variation of rim lighting is when the subject is in three quarters profile with most of their face turned away from the camera. The light is positioned to highlight the profile, allowing some to spill across and illuminate the eye nearest the camera.

Butterfly lighting is a lighting pattern where the main light in front of the subject is placed above and pointing down on the subject's face. This creates a small, butterfly-shaped shadow just below the subject's nose, making the cheekbones and facial structure more prominent.

This type of lighting was popular with Hollywood studios during the 20th century and used for creating studio portraits of their most glamorous and beautiful actresses. Careful placement of the light is required if you want to use it. If it's too high, shadows under the subject's eyes are emphasised; too low and you lose the 'butterfly' shadow. A reflector can be placed low down out of view of the camera to bounce the light back up into the face and soften the overall effect.

Split lighting divides the face into equal halves with one half brighter than the other. The light is positioned at 90 degrees to the left or right of the subject so the only part of the shadowed area lit is the eye.

This half-shadow effect can draw attention to facial symmetry so it's best used with subjects with symmetrical faces. Soft lighting is preferred in such situations. When the light source is hard and the shadowed area is relatively dark, this type of lighting is often used to create dramatic or moody shots of the type popular for musicians and artists.

Rembrandt lighting is a classical lighting pattern that aims to achieve a flattering sense of depth in portraits.

Right: This portrait shows the position of the main light for butterfly lighting. Note the discrete, butterfly-shaped shadow below the subject's nose. (Source: Camera House.)

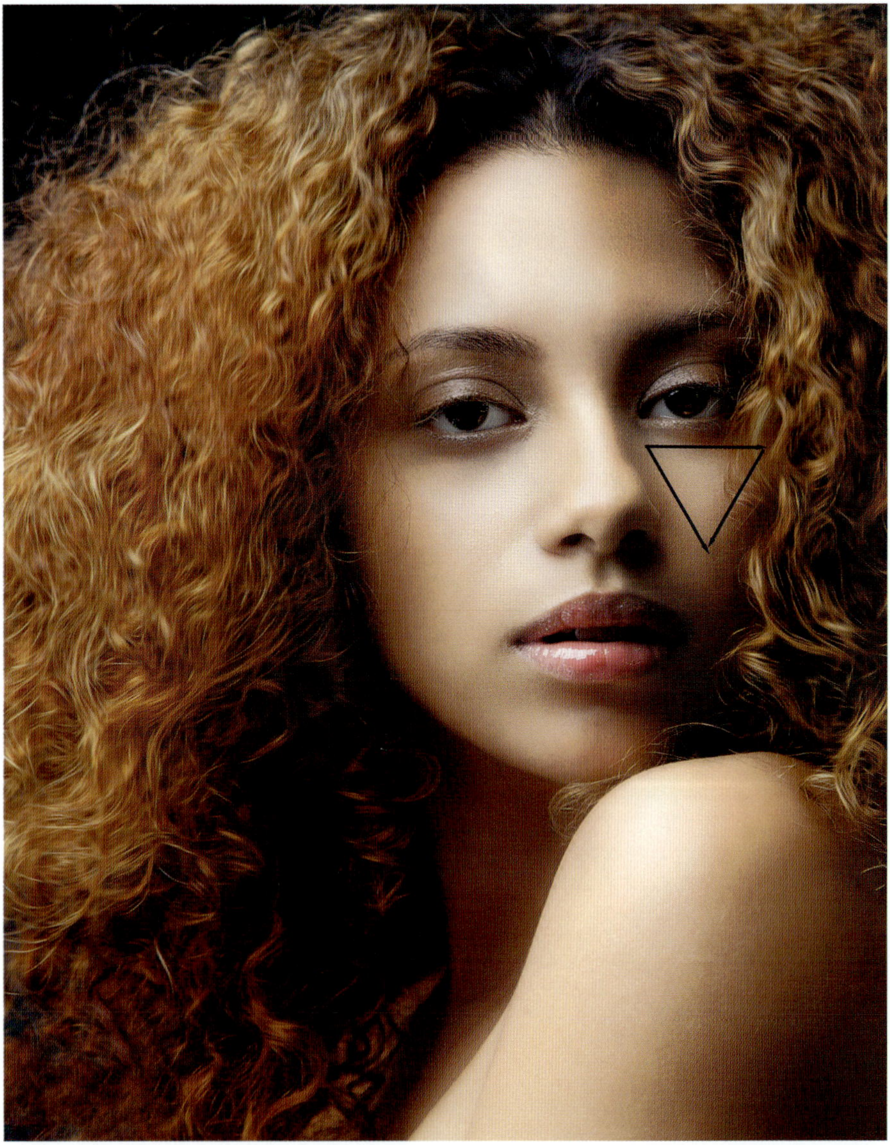

Rembrandt lighting arranges the studio lights to illuminate a triangular area on the subject's cheek, as shown in the outlined space in this illustration.

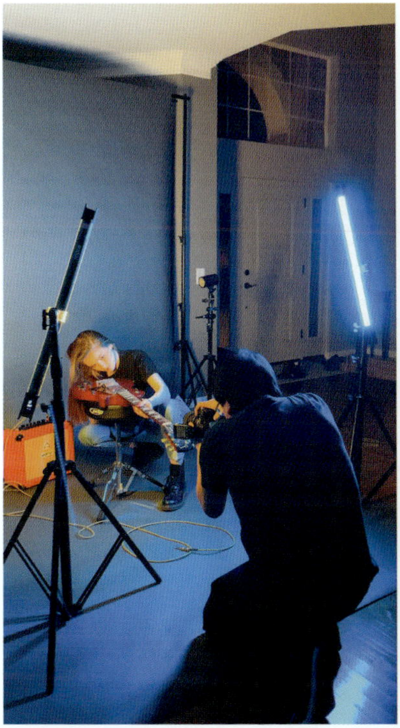

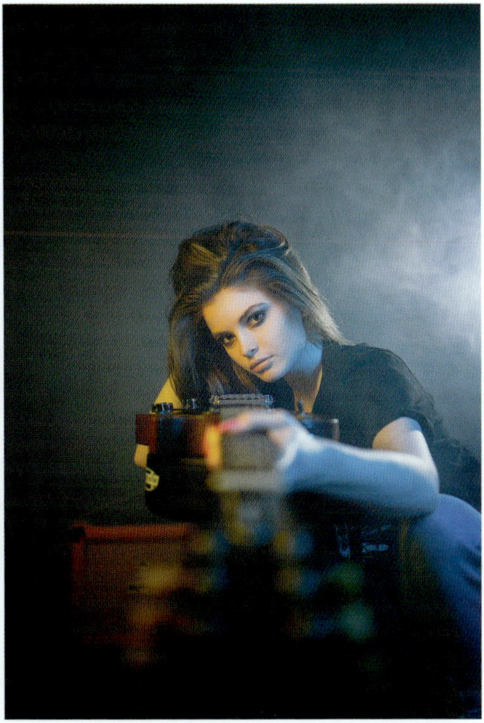

Studio portraits require more than just dedicated light sources; the photographer's imagination can create arresting results from relatively simple setups. (Source: Camera House.)

The light is positioned so it falls mainly on one side of the subject's face but spills across to illuminate a triangular area on the opposite cheek. This pattern best suited to subjects with slim faces. When the light is soft it can also be used to downplay wrinkles.

As with other lighting patterns, the intensity and spread of the light are regulated by moving the light source towards or away from the subject. Traditionally, the triangle should be no wider than the subject's eye and no longer than the nose, although this rule can be more flexible, especially with soft lighting.

When the key triangle is too big (i.e. it spills over onto the nose, forehead and/or hairline) it means the light is too close to the front of the subject. If the triangle is too narrow, the light is too far to the side of the subject and will probably cause the nose to cast a longer shadow. If it's too short, the light is too high or low, which can create shadows underneath the eyes or poor shadow definition along the jaw line.

Finding inspiration

All the lighting techniques outlined in this chapter are equally suitable for shooting stills and video and, as a result, you can find inspiration by looking out for the different types of lighting used in films and TV programs (including advertisements). The 'classic' movies of the 20th century often provide the best examples, especially if they were filmed in black and white.

Don't be afraid to experiment with your lighting angles. Each subject is unique, so it's worth making an effort to ensure you're lighting them in the most flattering way – or in a way that ties in with your creative objective.

Useful links

What you need in your photography studio
www.bit.ly/38uAMar

The integrity of imagining
www.bit.ly/3wZSY3K

CHAPTER 7

Flash and LED lights

Electronic flash is such a convenient and easy-to-use light source that even basic cameras come with built-in flash tubes. In contrast, most smartphones have built-in LED lights that can be used for taking still pictures as well as shooting movies. Both light sources are largely interchangeable and both normally illuminate subjects directly from the camera, which can be problematic, as outlined in the box on the next page.

Built-in flashes may be easy to use, but their results are often disappointing. They're also totally unsuitable for use when shooting video.

Because the small Zenon tubes have low light output they can't illuminate anything beyond a metre or two away. Close to the subject their light can be quite harsh and they often produce red eyes in human subjects (an example can be found in Chapter 2) or yellow/green eyes in dogs and cats.

Accessory flashguns are generally more powerful and versatile as well as providing a wider range of adjustments. They can be used either attached to the camera's hot shoe or held apart from the camera on a stand or by a co-operative assistant.

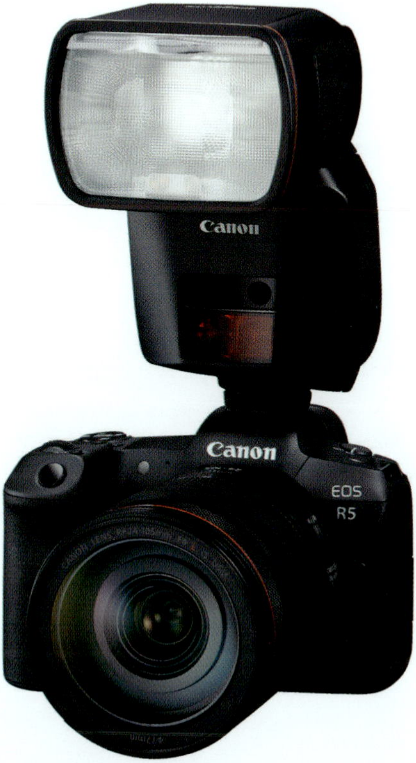

An electronic flashgun like the Canon Speedlite EL-1model shown on this professional camera provides a convenient, portable and very versatile source of light for taking photographs at weddings and events as well as for portrait shots.

Many also have adjustable heads for 'bouncing' the light (see box on the opposite page) and most come with translucent diffuser panels that fit over the flash tube to soften and spread the light. You can also diffuse the light by covering the flash tube with a single layer of tissue.

Portrait photographers usually restrict the flash power, depending on the distance from the flash to the subject (accounting for the inverse-square law). Most cameras allow you to reduce the light by a stop or two, to prevent subjects near the camera from being over-exposed.

Direct lighting

Regardless of how it's produced, shining a bright light on a subject's face creates **flat** lighting with few, if any, shadows to add interest and bring out the subject's character. Interestingly, flat lighting is often used for portraits of children and professional models where character is less important than the appearance of 'beauty'.

Flat lighting downplays wrinkles and other skin blemishes and also de-emphasise deeply-set eyes and pouches below eyes. It can also work if your subject has acne, other blemishes or wrinkles.

Unfortunately, flat lighting often produces bland, uninteresting portraits that don't reveal a subject's character. Wrinkles and shadows often bring the face to life.

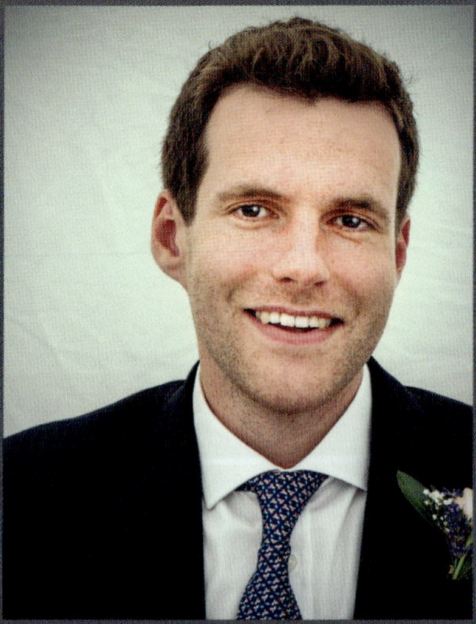

On-camera flash can flatten the facial contours and prevent the subject's character from showing through. While some people might consider this image successful, use of off-camera flash could reveal facial contours that would make a more interesting portrait.

Bounce flash

Another way to reduce flash intensity is to 'bounce' the flash light off a white or beige-coloured wall or ceiling. You'll need a separate flashgun with a swivelling head to attach to the camera.

Fit a translucent 'diffuser' panel (or put a single layer of facial tissue over the flash head and keep it in place with a rubber band) to further soften the light. Some accessory flashguns also provide coloured diffusers to add a warmer or cooler tone to the light from the flash. Warming diffusers can be especially useful when shooting outdoors on cloudy days.

Using bounce flash lets you use the normal through-the-lens (TTL) metering options provided by your camera. However, you may need to take a couple of test shots to see if the bounce set-up delivers the results you want.

It's not uncommon for shots to be under-exposed when the flash is bounced off a surface that is a long way

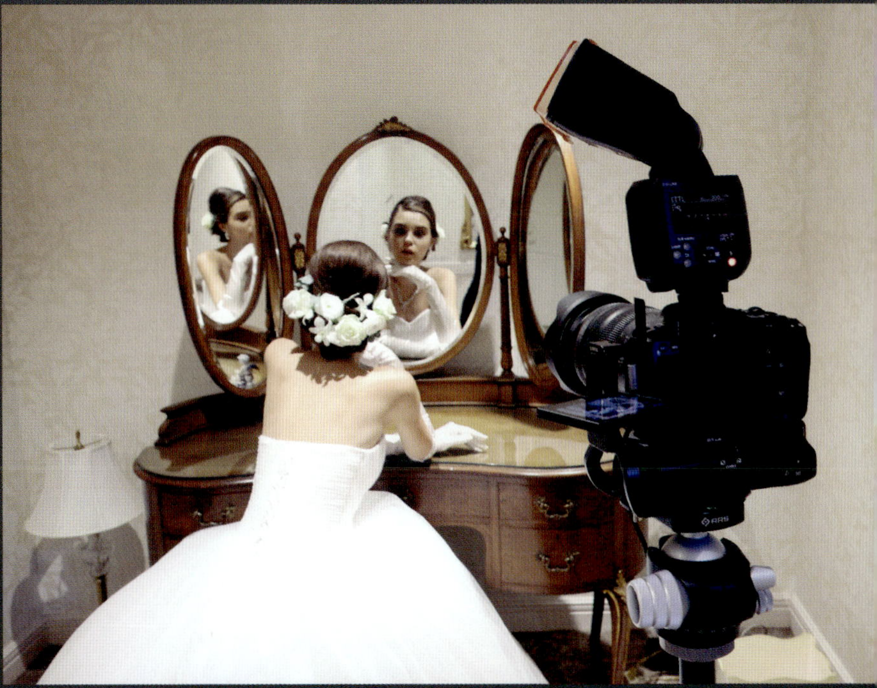

Bouncing the light from the flash off the light-toned ceiling softened the light and minimised the risk of the flash being reflected in the mirrors. (Source: Canon Australia.)

from the subject. By the same token, if the bounce surface is too close, the shot is likely to be over-exposed and the advantages of bouncing the light are lost.

It's easy to compensate for too-bright or too-dark flash exposures. Stop the lens aperture down if the flash is too bright; open the aperture a stop if the flash fill doesn't add enough light.

Below: Bounced light from an on-camera flash can augment ambient indoor lighting without compromising existing lighting. TTL metering should be able to calculate the best exposure settings for the camera. (Source: Canon Australia.)

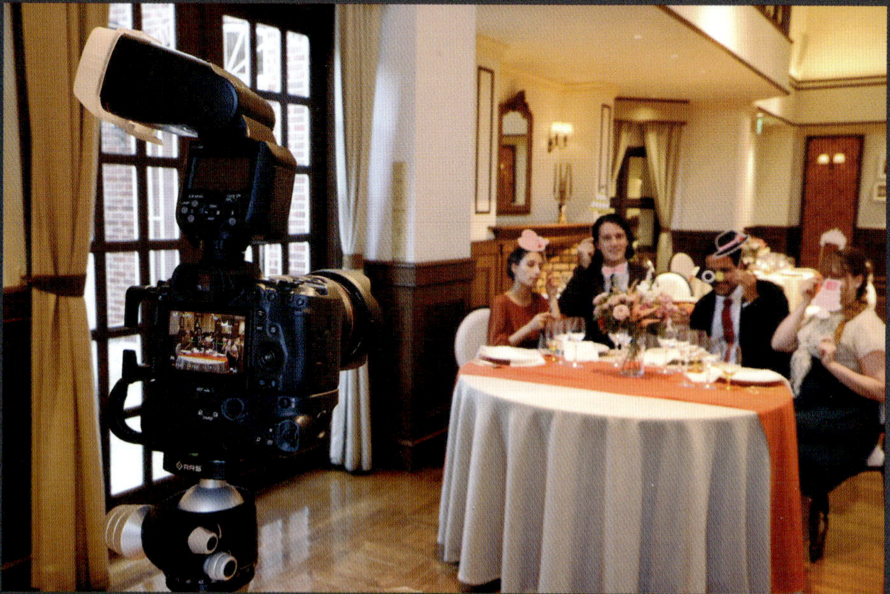

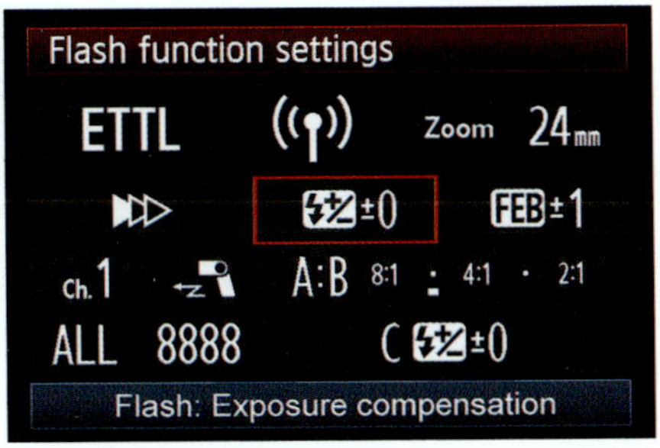

A typical camera menu page showing flash settings with exposure compensation highlighted. This setting is changed to a negative value to reduce the strength of the light from the flash. The FEB setting to the right is for setting flash exposure bracketing values.

The flashgun may also be held away from the camera to create a more interesting light distribution. Off-camera flashguns can be held in the photographer's hand or placed on a stand and fired by either light from the on-camera flash or a remote trigger.

Several flashguns can be used at different distances from the subject, allowing complex professional set-ups to be achieved with relatively simple and affordable equipment. Reducing the flash output reduces recycle times and allows more flexibility with modifiers like filters and diffusers as well as for bouncing the light (see box).

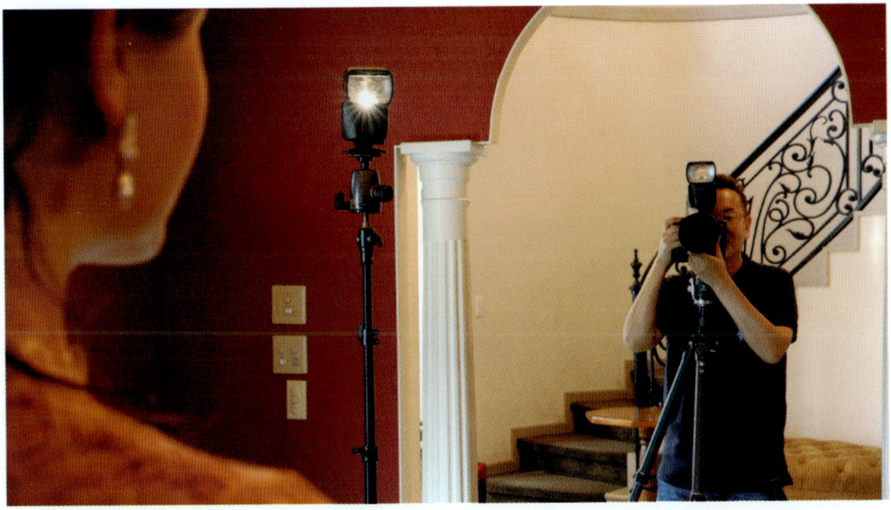

A second flashgun on a stand away from the camera can produce a more natural-looking balance between subject and ambient lighting and prevent the subject's face from appearing flat. (Source: Canon Australia.)

The main downside of flash is that you can't see how well the shot worked until after it has been taken. In addition, flash can't be used for recording video clips.

The light output from most electronic flashguns is close enough in colour to normal daylight so you shouldn't need to adjust white balance settings.

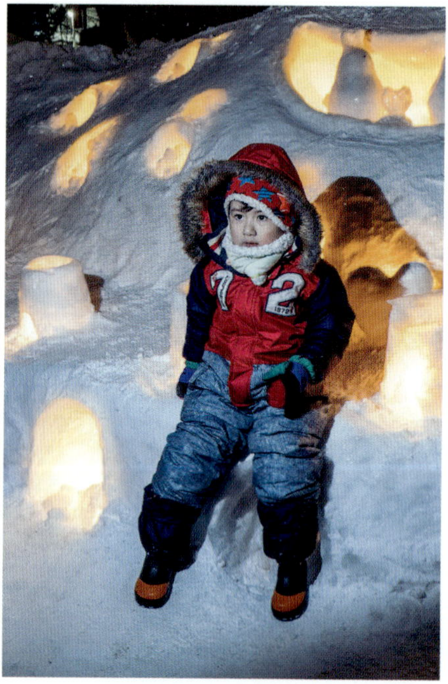

The Night Portrait mode in an entry-level camera or smartphone should balance the flash output to provide fill-in light for the subject's face while also recording the background. Note: Since flash light only travels for a metre or two, distant backgrounds are under-exposed.

Where a camera fails to produce the right colour balance, try using the Flash pre-set in the camera's white balance sub-menu.

Fill-in flash

One of the most effective ways to use a camera's built-in flash is for 'filling in' shadowed areas in harsh lighting, such as you would find on a beach or a snowy slope when the sun is high in a cloudless sky. Flash fill can also be handy when shooting backlit portraits (with the main light source behind the subject).

Photographers can also take advantage of the extremely brief exposures produced by electronic flash to 'freeze' subjects in motion for action portraits. Night portraits like the ones shown on this page are particularly good examples of this capability.

Many simple cameras and smartphones include 'Night Portrait' shooting modes that can balance ambient light levels with the amount of flash light the system provides. These modes often work well but red-eye reduction may be needed for subjects close to the camera.

In well-lit environments you usually need to set the camera to 'force' the flash to fire. This setting is usually indicated with a flash icon. Cameras usually default to a flash ratio near 1:1, which means the flash output is equivalent to the ambient lighting.

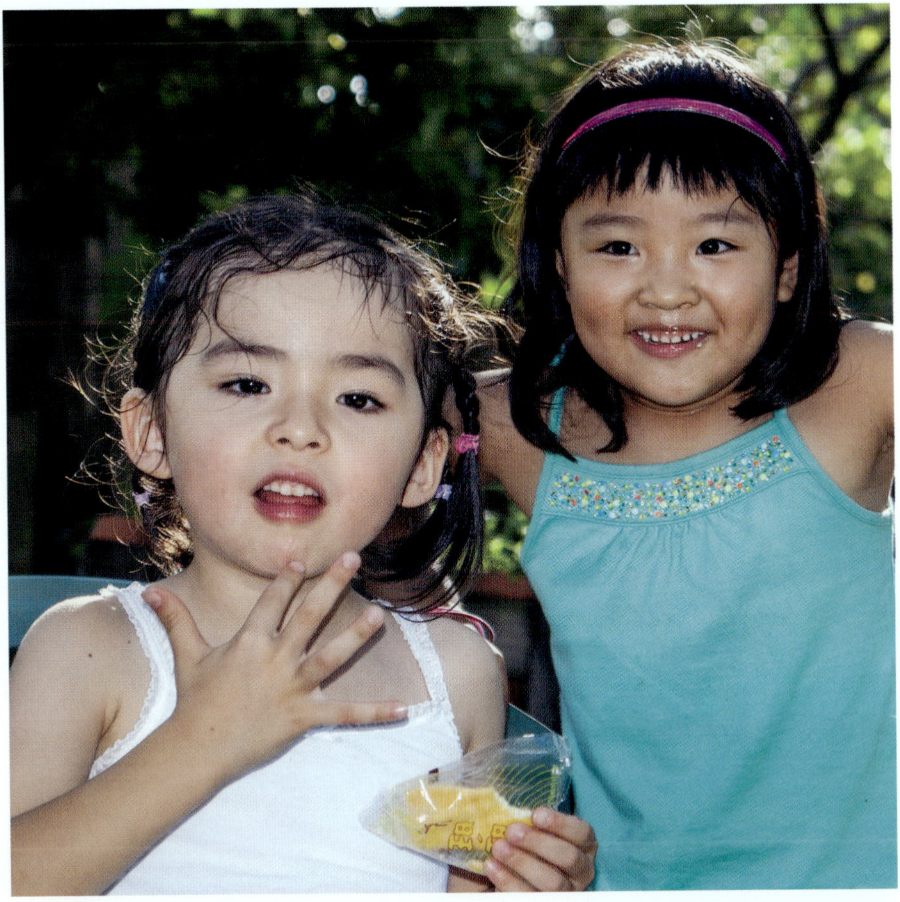

Flash fill is useful when shooting backlit portraits, particularly of lively children. The flat lighting is less of a problem than it is with older subjects.

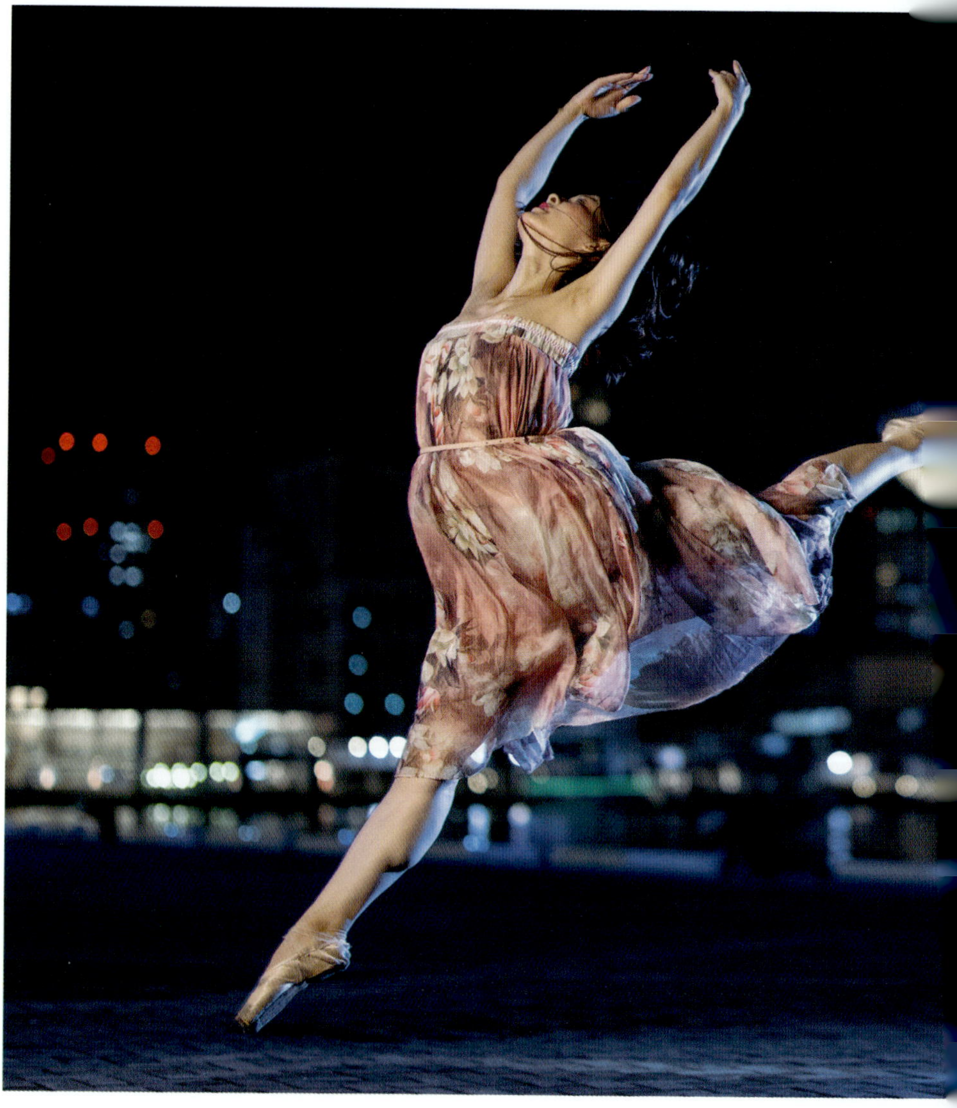

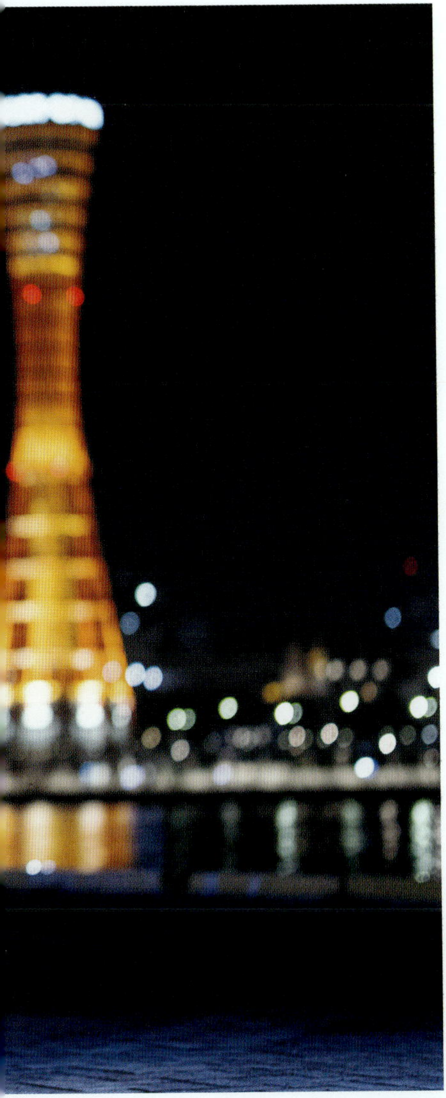

One of the best ways to use electronic flash is for action portraits like the one shown here, which was taken with a Canon EOS R5 camera and Speedlite E-L1 flashgun; 50mm focal length, 1/100 second at f/1.2. (Source: Canon Australia.)

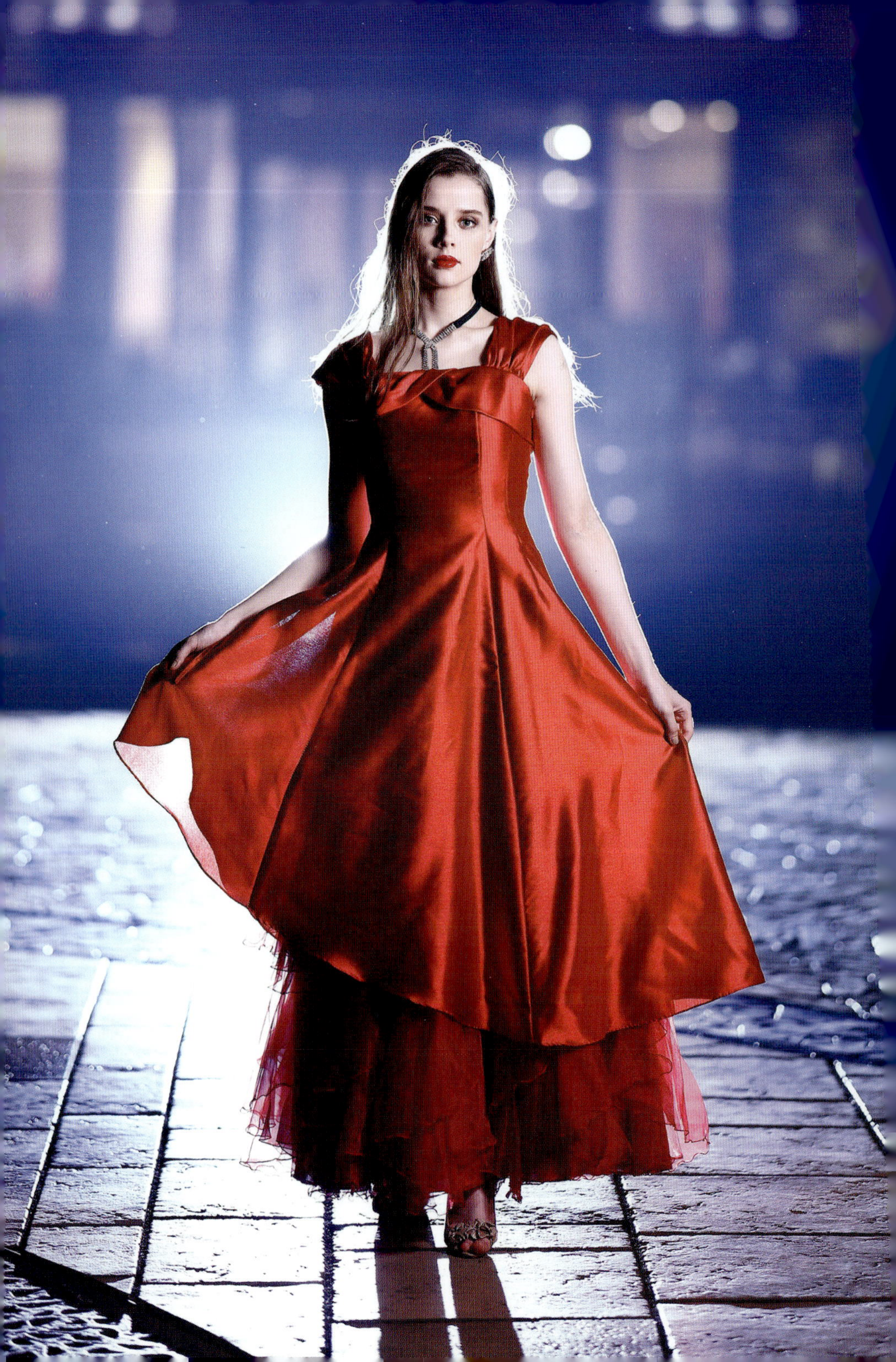

The challenge is to balance the flash exposure to ensure enough light falls on the subject to illuminate darker shadows – but not so much as to completely over-expose the subject. We suggest starting with -1EV of flash compensation and dial the EV settings back further in 1/3EV steps until a satisfactory balance is achieved.

Flashes that use TTL (through the lens) metering can often achieve a balance automatically, although they may be influenced by the metering mode you choose. We recommend using either the Aperture-priority AE or Manual shooting mode plus the multi-pattern metering mode.

LED panels

LED (light-emitting diode) panels are becoming increasingly popular with serious enthusiasts through to high-level professionals because of their versatility. Panels are available in different sizes from tiny ones that cost less than $50 and can be used with smartphones through to panels designed for studio use that cost more than $500 and are more than half a metre wide.

In most cases, LED lights can be used instead of flash, where they have three main advantages:

1. They have relatively low power consumption, which means they tend to run 'cool';

2. The photographer can see the effects of the light in-camera before taking the photo;

3. The photographer can use the same light for shooting stills and video.

LED panels also have light outputs that are close to natural daylight and more sophisticated, bi-colour panels provide separate settings for daylight (5500K) and indoor (3200K) lighting. Unlike flash, LED lights don't cause the iris in the subject's eyes to dilate, removing the possibility of the dreaded 'red-eye' phenomenon. Instead, they let you see more of the iris and the eyes' colour, which can produce more attractive results.

However, while LED panels are great light sources for shooting video, they can't be used for 'freezing' action. Electronic flash is always superior for those shots.

Left: Professional photographers often combine fill-in flash with other forms of lighting, especially at night, as shown in this fashion portrait. (Source: Canon Australia.)

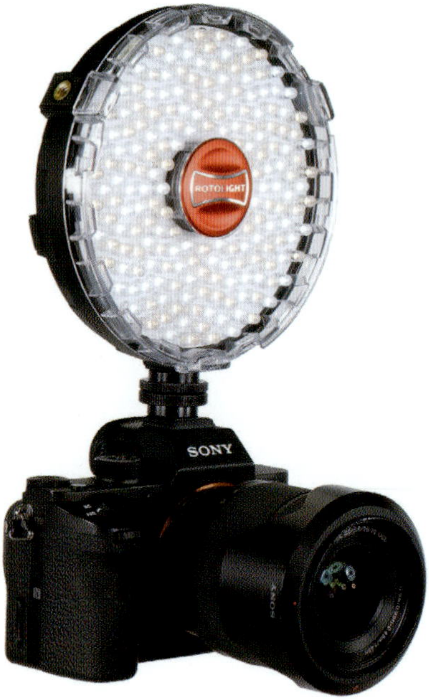

The portable LED light shown above can operate as either a continuous LED light source or a high-speed flash. It can be attached to the camera's hot-shoe (as shown) or remotely activated from a separate transmitter.

Small LED panels usually include a hot shoe for on-camera mounting, where they draw power from the camera's battery and can be controlled via the camera menu. Higher-featured panels have adjustments for controlling the output of the light, just like those on accessory flashguns.

Many include Kelvin settings for controlling the colour of the light output. Some also accept diffusers and coloured gels for 'warming' or 'cooling' the tone of the ambient lighting. These colour adjustments can range from very subtle through to obvious colour effects.

High-powered LED panels designed for studio use require separate power sources. That can mean additional cords that could present a tripping hazard. However, these panels can be fitted with all the professional light modifiers that are found in studio set-ups, making them a nice alternative to studio flash.

Useful links

Low-light photography
www.bit.ly/3Gwm0fO

The art of anticipation
www.bit.ly/3wVcqi8

CHAPTER 8

Children and families

Photographing children can be challenging – and the challenges vary with different age levels. Fortunately, today's equipment makes it relatively easy to obtain attractive portrait shots so a lot depends on the skill of the photographer and, above all else, their ability to communicate effectively with their subjects.

Attending to equipment before the shoot makes it easier to concentrate on working with subjects and keeping them cheerful and co-operative. The following list provides tips on how to set up your camera for a shoot:

1. **Choose an appropriate lens**. Longer lenses are best if you want to fill the frame with your subject(s), while wider lenses can make it easier to capture children in a favoured environment. A 24-105mm or 24-135mm (35mm equivalent) zoom lens gives you scope for shifting quickly from close-up to wide view while tracking active subjects.

2. Use Program AE or Aperture priority mode for maximum flexibility. Alternatively, select the 'Portrait' mode from the auto pre-sets to provide some separation between the subject and the background.

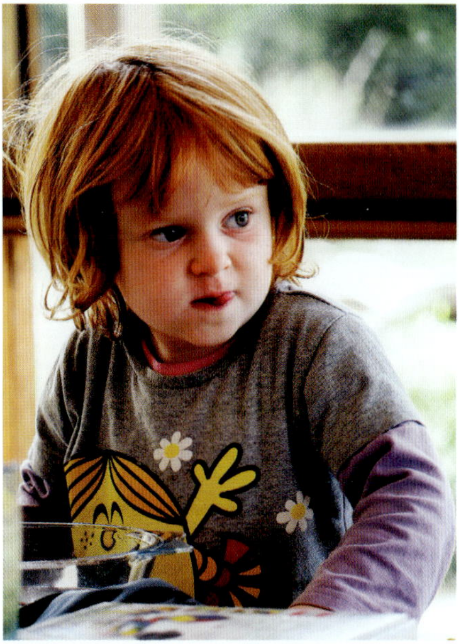

Longer focal lengths – in this case 200mm – give you a working distance that lets you fill the frame with the subject without attracting attention. Such lenses are best for candid shots like this one, although they tend to compress perspective, making background objects appear closer to the subject than they actually are. M4/3 camera with 117mm focal length, ISO 800, 1/100 second at f/5.3.

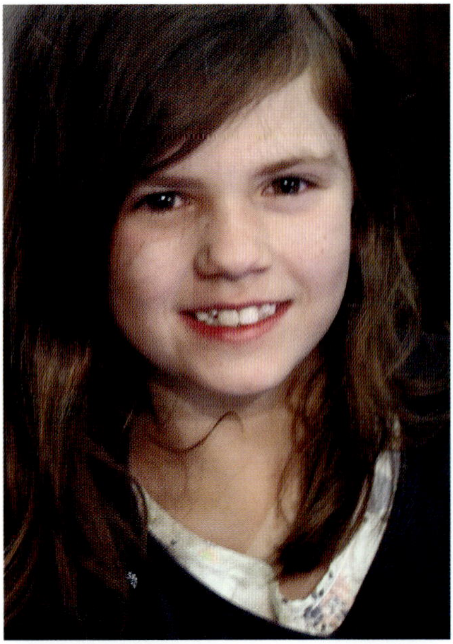

Effective stabilisation plus a high ISO setting was required for this indoor portrait, which was taken without flash. Shot at ISO 1600 with an 85mm lens; 1/10 second at f/4.2.

When using Aperture priority mode, start with an aperture of f/5.6 and adjust it up and down, depending on the shutter speeds measured by the camera. Open the aperture to f/2.8 to blur distracting backgrounds, but be aware that the plane of focus becomes narrow at wider apertures.

3. ISO settings will depend on whether you're shooting indoors or out and the levels of the ambient lighting. A good strategy is to set the ISO to Auto and then restrict the uppermost end of the usable range.

4. Optical stabilisation is highly advantageous, either in the camera or the lens. It's best s to have it in both, as long as they work together. Digital stabilisation crops the frame and is best avoided – except for shooting video.

5. Check the shutter speeds the camera is choosing. If you're not using stabilised equipment, use shutter speeds at or above 1/200 second. With stabilised gear, the claimed stabilisation represents the **most** compensation you can gain. For example, if the camera or lens claims four stops of shake correction, you could reduce the shutter speed to 1/25 second – as long as your shooting technique is up to scratch.

6. Flash is best avoided. If you must use flash, diffuse it or bounce it off a light-toned wall or ceiling. Remember the colour of the reflector affects the colour of the light that falls on the subject.

7. Focus settings depend on whether subjects are static or mobile. Single-shot AF is best for seated subjects, while continuous AF is safest for active, moving children. Note that using continuous AF drains the camera's battery faster than single AF mode.

Select a multi-point AF mode plus tracking AF to keep moving subjects in focus. If the camera offers face and eye detection, make sure it is enabled.

8. Shooting raw files gives you the greatest scope for post-capture editing and the best chance of obtaining great, printable photographs.

Age-related tips

Different shooting strategies apply to different age groups and whether you are photographing individuals alone or with siblings or friends. Family groups also need different handling.

Newborns are a special category and photographers must prioritise the well being of the subject. Always involve parents in the shoot, especially when you need to move the baby into a new position to capture a different angle.

Most newborn shots are taken when babies are between one and two weeks old – a time when they spend much of the day asleep. This makes them easy to pose. Keep lighting soft and gentle, favouring natural illumination over artificial light sources. Avoid flash as it can startle the baby.

Keep setups simple and move in close, filling the frame with the subject. Include close-ups of the baby's feet and hands. If the baby is awake, try turning it onto its tummy and shooting from the front. Take shots of the baby in a parent's arms as well as a family group.

Toddlers are beginning to explore the world and many are on the move from the moment they awake to when they fall asleep. Plan your shoot for a time when they're fresh, happy and active.

Natural lighting is best for this group and if they're old enough to be allowed to run about outdoors, this is the best place to photograph them. You'll probably need a longer lens – an extended-range zoom provides the most flexibility. Look for opportunities to take backlit shots.

Painting sessions can produce great shots while allowing the child to have a lot of fun. Parent-child interactions are much more meaningful than static, posed shots.

Pop the child on Dad's shoulders, sit them on a swing and get it moving; give them something to do. Distract them with food. (Look up cake-smash photos of toddlers on the web for some ideas.)

Pre-teens are old enough to participate actively in a photo shoot and follow directions. Make your shoot a fun activity, including props like favourite toys and/or pets. Giving subjects something to do is a useful strategy.

So is photographing them with pets or while they're sharing games or engaging in active games.

Most kids also enjoy showing off. Ask them to show you their bike, skateboard, scooter and demonstrate their skills. Building Lego, setting up train or racing car sets, playing board games like Snakes & Ladders, UNO or Jenga can also yield some great spontaneous action shots.

Older children could try using the camera to take pictures of their parents or siblings.

In short, allow your subjects to play, interact and just be themselves. Then follow their lead and photograph the action as it happens.

Adolescents require sensitive handling as they are beginning to be aware of themselves as individuals with distinctive characteristics. Some of the best shots

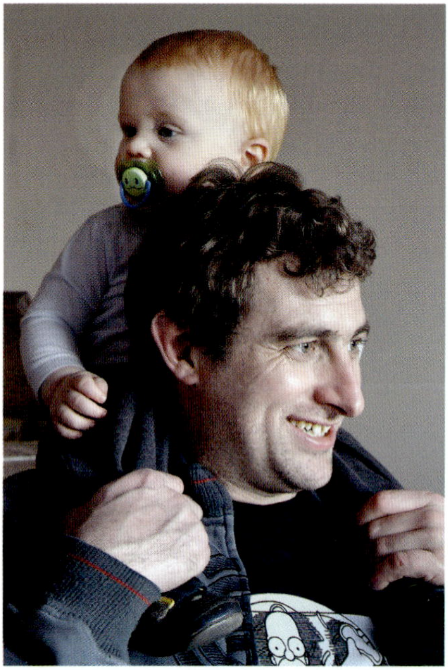

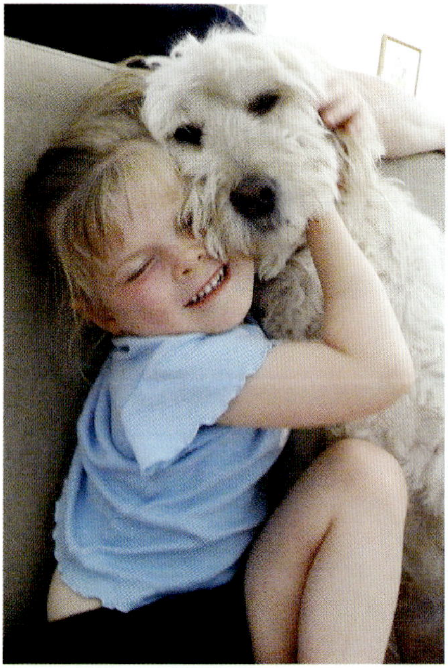

Left: Toddlers are often more relaxed when being held by a parent. Take advantage of situations like this to grab a few quick shots, particularly if the child is reluctant to be photographed.

Right: Many pre-teens are happy to pose for photos with a well-loved pet.

of this age group can be taken when they're unaware of your camera.

Most react positively to a little guidance on how to pose, although the guiding principle is to allow them to behave normally. Embrace their individuality and use it wherever possible.

Teenagers often feel self-conscious. They don't want to be patronised or treated like a child. Effective communication is the key, which means the best results come about when they are in control of the clothes they wear, the places they are photographed in and their facial expressions.

Work as quickly as you can to keep shoots brief, interesting and non-confrontational. Start a casual conversation if you can to make them feel at ease. Jokes can help to lighten

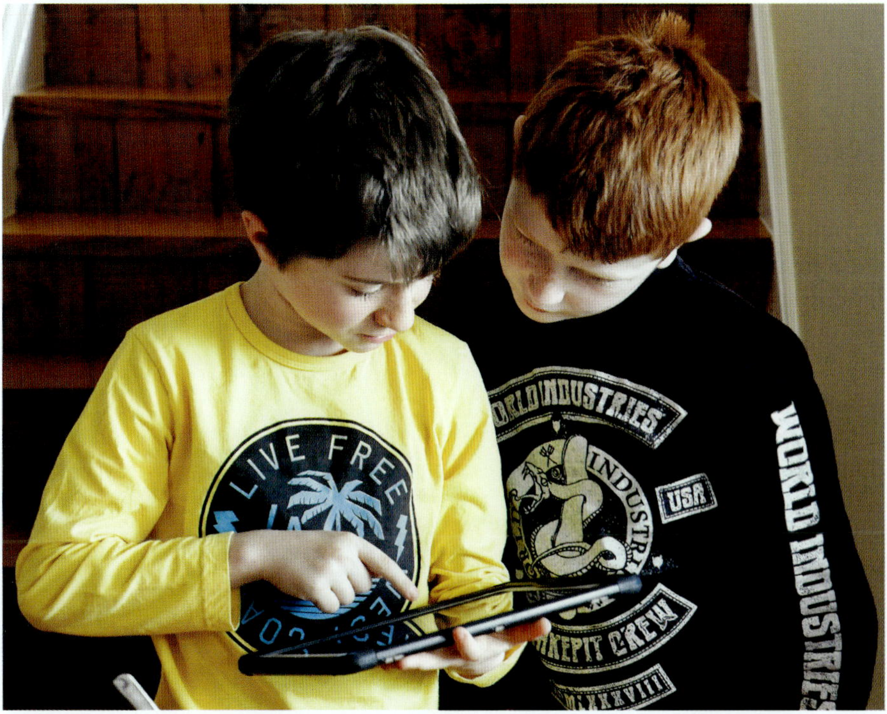

Shared games can provide opportunities to photograph pre-teens who might otherwise be reluctant subjects. A short (85mm) telephoto lens allowed a good working distance so the shot could be taken without distracting the subjects.

the atmosphere – but only if they come naturally. Like most adults, teens can see quickly when interactions are forced and artificial.

Family groups

Families come in different sizes and age groups so each shooting session needs to be tackled as a one-off adventure. With small groups of between three and five people, posing is usually easy. Triangular compositions often work well with the tallest members in the centre and shorter ones on each side. Toddlers and babies are easiest to photograph when they're sitting on a parent's (or older sibling's) lap.

Whether it's a snapshot to commemorate the large family reunion or a family portrait for Christmas emails, large groups of people can be tricky to organise for a photograph. Natural light is the easiest to work with so you should try to set the group up outdoors.

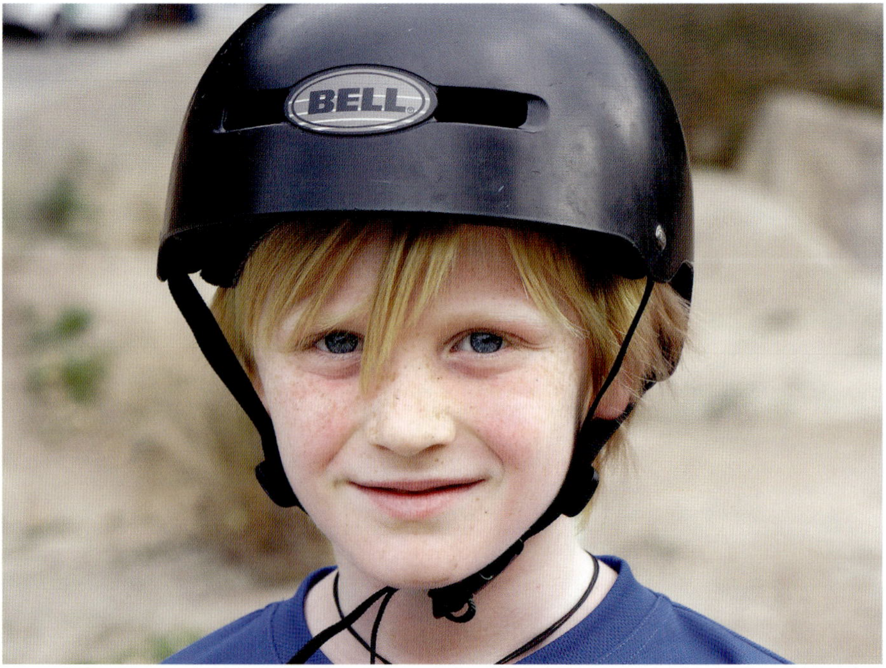

Older pre-teens should be encouraged to be themselves.

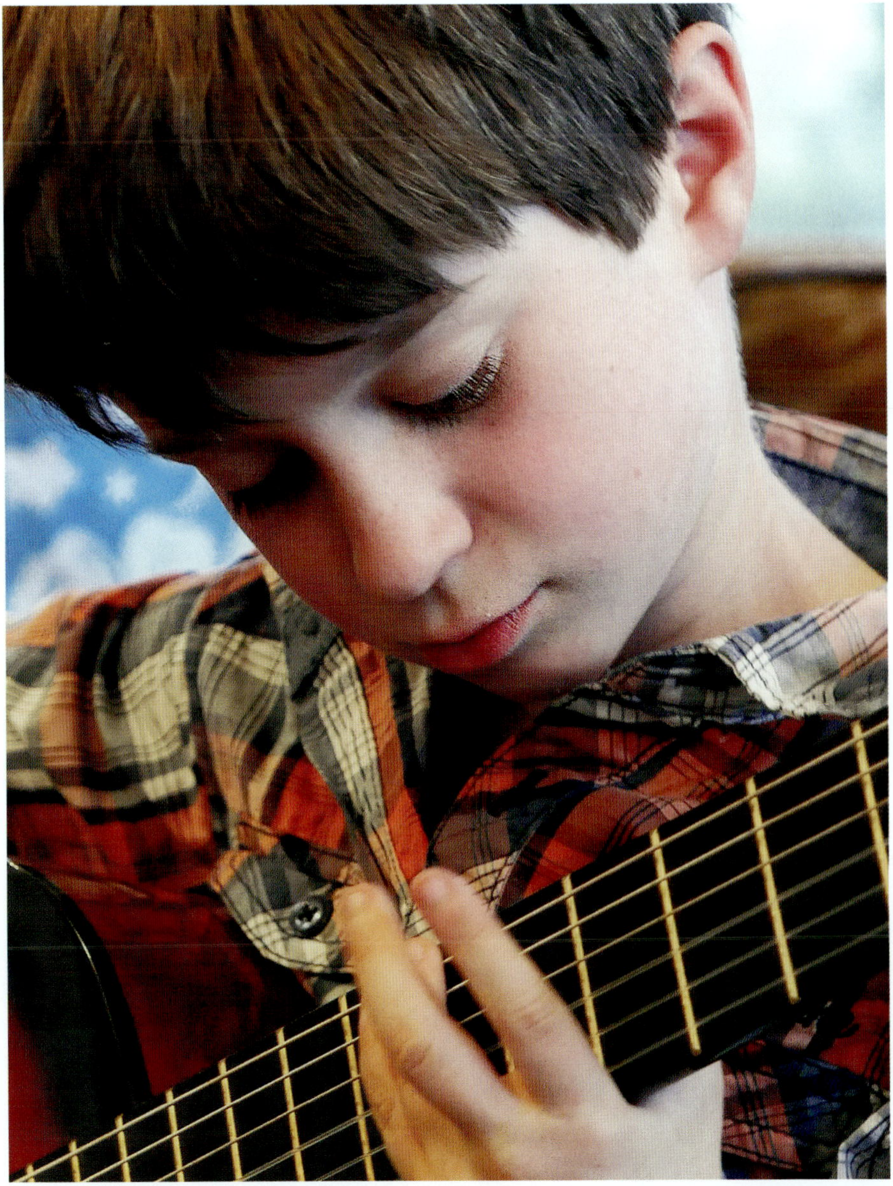

Capture teenagers and pre-teens with an instrument if their interests are musical.

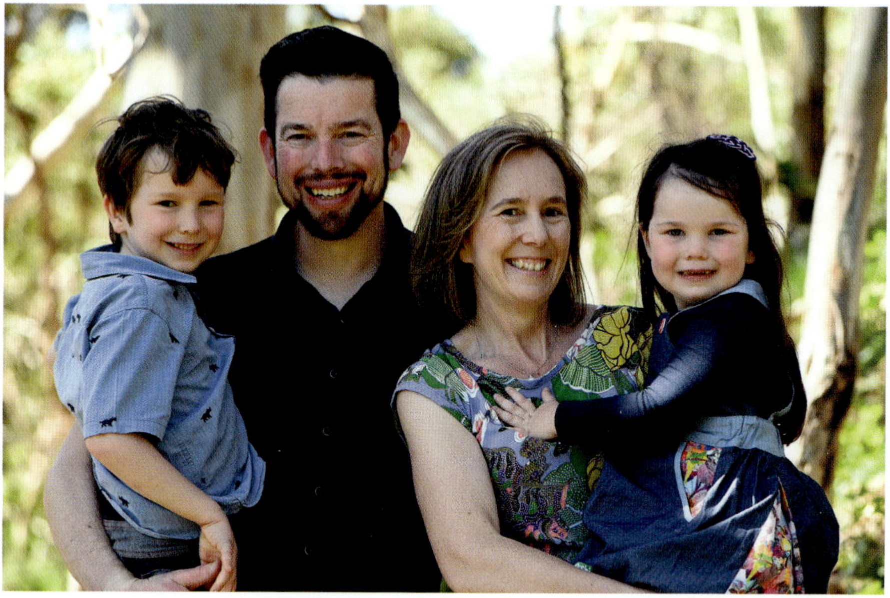

A moderate telephoto focal length and high ISO setting made it easy to fit this typical family group into the frame and cope with the soft and subdued lighting associated with afternoon shade. No flash was required, which made it easier to capture natural responses to the photographer. (Source: Catherine Leo Photography.)

Watch out for harsh shadows in bright sunlight; the gentler light of late afternoon produce much better results.

Use a wide angle lens and consolidate the group so everyone fits into the frame: smaller children should go in front with the tallest adults at the rear. Stopping down the lens to f/5.6 with medium-sized groups or f/8 with large groups should give you an adequate depth of focus. Reduce the aperture even more in very bright conditions. Consider using flash fill with moderately large groups.

Mounting your camera on a tripod gives you more freedom to direct moderately-sized groups. For really large groups, you may need to climb up on a ladder or take the shots from a balcony or deck above the crowd to fit everybody in.

Make sure everyone is visible; it's too easy for toddlers to get lost in the sea of legs or shy people to hide behind others. Ask if they can see you, warning that if they can't, the camera won't see them.

Fill the frame wherever possible, especially with larger groups. Remember, stacking people in layers allows you to fit more heads into the frame both vertically and horizontally.

Before snapping the photo, take a few seconds to gather everyone's attention and ensure they're looking at the camera lens, not something else. Asking them to say 'cheese' is an old standard; asking them instead to say 'silly Billy' is more likely to raise a grin.

Taking a series of shots increases the likelihood of most people in the shot looking in the right direction and having their eyes open. In 50 shots, you might end up with three or four where everyone looks great.

An attractive backdrop is nice, but large objects like trees or buildings can obscure faces and cast unflattering shadows. The trick is being able to find a shady spot that won't cast uneven or unflattering shadows, but still shields the group from the sun.

Useful links

How to shoot and edit group portraits
www.bit.ly/3wZfIST

Montaging the past into the present
www.bit.ly/pg32-23

CHAPTER 9

Weddings and community events

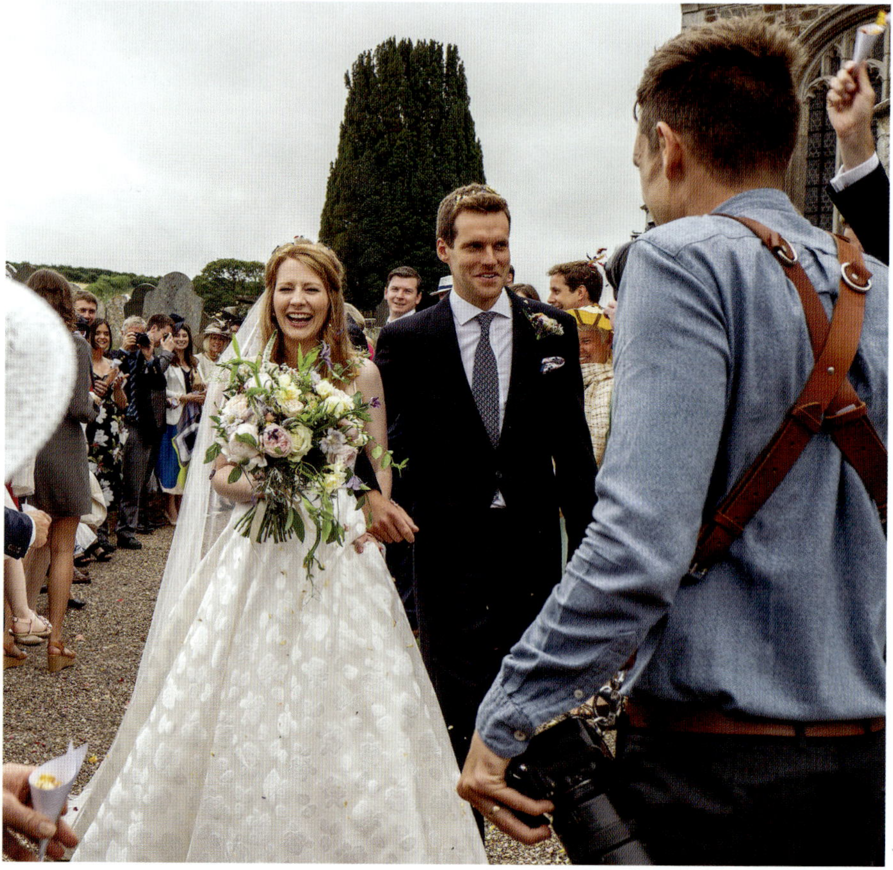

The professional photographer shown here is earning his living; even close family members should respect this and not get in the way.

Most couples hire a professional photographer to cover their weddings, with the aim of producing an album of shots that cover the action plus a few special photos for framing. But sometimes family members or friends with appropriate gear and the knowledge of how to use it are roped in to either substitute for a professional or take additional snapshots for sharing.

A delicate balance exists when shooting alongside a hired professional. It's important to keep in mind that the pro is earning a living, while you should be on the sidelines.

Many pros don't mind a few amateurs taking photos at the event – as long as they don't try to replace them. As long as you mind your manners – and don't get in the pro's way – you should be able to take all the shots you need. You can also take advantage of the pro's ability to organise group shots; some pros even step aside once they've captured all the shots they need to allow relatives and friends to snap the group.

If you're the only photographer covering the wedding professionally, unless you're a close friend or family member, you probably need a legally binding contract, signed by the client. It should set out what photographs will be covered and what end products will be supplied to the client in the form of prints and albums. Where video is involved, similar details should also be included.

Signing a contract means the clients agree with the role you play and you agree to carry out the designated tasks and provide the goods and services the clients will receive. Signed documents provide protection to both parties, especially since there's money involved.

Most couples require the following scenes for a basic coverage of the wedding:

- Venue shots of the site of the ceremony, including the flowers and interior, and exterior details;
- Shots of people getting ready for the wedding;
- The arrival of the bridal party and their entrance to the venue;
- The exchange of vows and/or rings;
- The couple's first kiss as a married couple;
- Signing the marriage certificate;
- The couple leaving the venue surrounded by admiring guests;
- Group portraits of the couple with their attendants, the couple with both sets of parents, the couple with close family members, the couple with close friends;
- At the reception you'll need shots of the entrance of the couple, the high table group shot, toasts and speeches, cutting the cake and the first dance.

Most of these shots are best handled by the professional photographer – assuming there is one. But there's likely to be plenty of 'gaps' for others to fill in and that's where enthusiasts can make a real contribution.

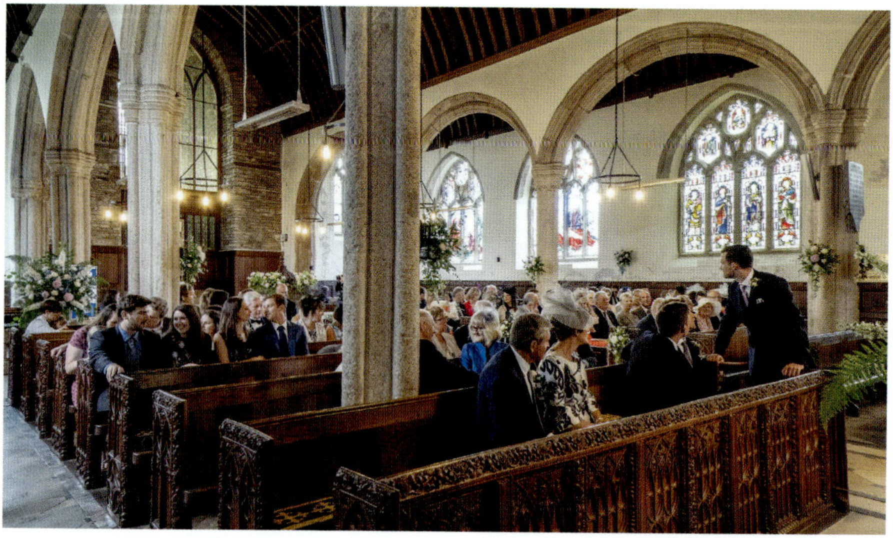

Most couples appreciate photographs taken in the venue while waiting for the wedding to begin. Since the professional photographer may have been busy at the time, snapshots like this can make a welcome addition to the overall coverage of the event.

Anything that records an impression of the day will help you produce a great set of pictures covering the event. Don't underestimate the importance of taking casual snapshots of family members and friends; these photos are often the most valued in the future, especially when they include elders in the family.

Community events

Keen photographers are often called to supply pictures of community-based events to sporting clubs, theatre groups and other functions run by local volunteers. These groups seldom have a budget to accommodate hiring a professional photographer so interested amateurs can make an important contribution.

Whether you're shooting for a sporting club, theatre group or organisation like the Scouts or Guides or even the local school or playgroup, it's important to know what the event is about, who will be present and when and where particular activities will be happening so you don't miss out important moments. It's essential to know what kinds of pictures the organisers want. With this information you can decide what equipment you will need and be prepared in advance.

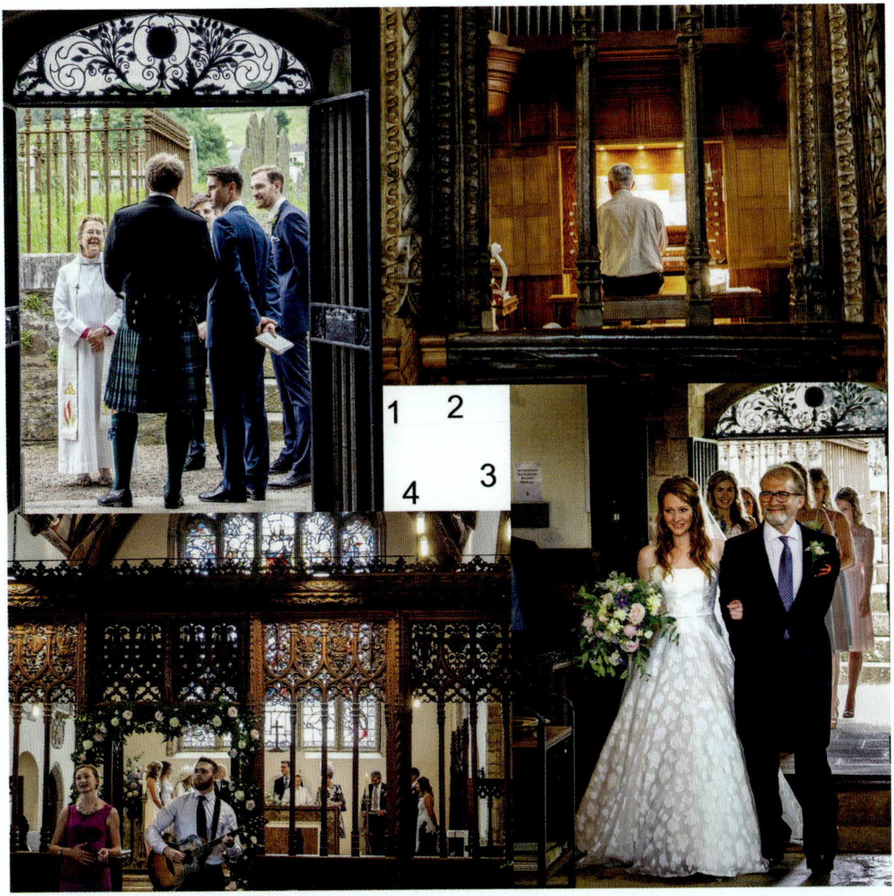

Four situations where non-professional photographers can make a contribution to the couple's 'memories' collection:

1: The groom and attendants converse with the celebrant before the bride arrives;

2: The organist playing the wedding march;

3: The arrival of the bride;

4: Entertainment while the registry is being signed (the official photographer should be covering this ceremony by shooting close-ups).

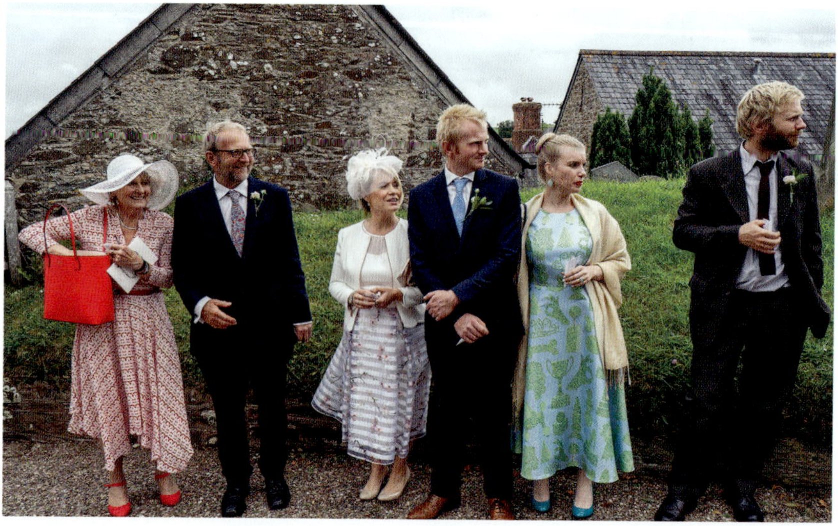

Casual snapshots of family members outside the venue are often missed by professional photographers ….

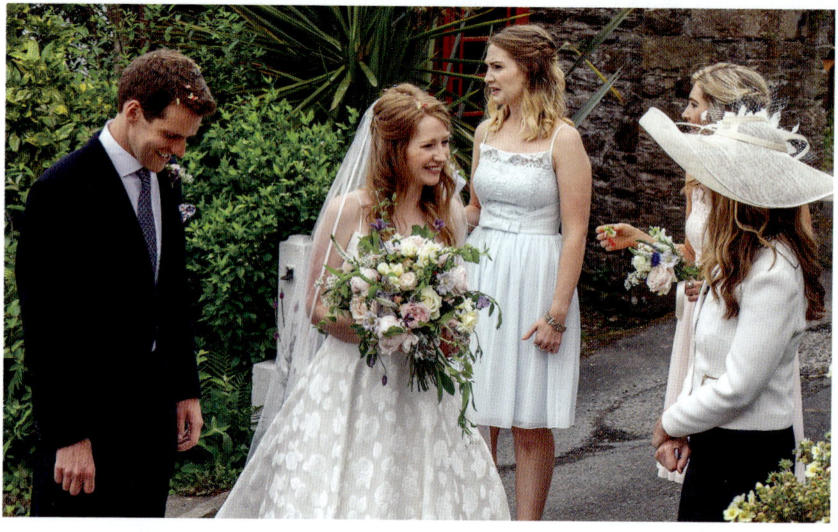

… yet they can provide pleasing recordings of the day's events.

Shooting tips

You don't need a load of fancy equipment to do wedding and event photography; it just needs to be suitable. Long lenses are ideal for sports photography; extended-range zooms work well when covering events that require you to shoot from different angles and produce both wide and close-up views.

Backup equipment is useful for your peace of mind. Using two cameras, each with a different lens, also saves you from having to switch lenses regularly. Many wedding and event photographers standardise on two fast zooms: a 24-70mm and a 70-200mm (in 35mm focal length equivalent).

Fast (f/2.8 maximum aperture) lenses are advantageous but if your camera performs well between ISO 800 and ISO 3200 you'll be able to use these higher sensitivities in relatively dim lighting. Built-in stabilisation – either in the camera body or the lens, or both – provides additional flexibility to shoot without additional light sources in poorly-lit rooms. It also provides better-balanced exposures when taking photographs of the venue and for photographing larger groups.

Accessory lights may be needed when working indoors. Also check for colour casts and adjust the camera's white balance to compensate. Most recent cameras have a 'keep white' auto white balance setting that can suppress unwanted colour casts; but you still need to check that it's effective.

Use on-camera flash to fill-in heavy shadows in backlit situations and when working indoors; but make sure you have diffusers and/or reflectors to soften harsh lighting. Check Chapter 6 for more information.

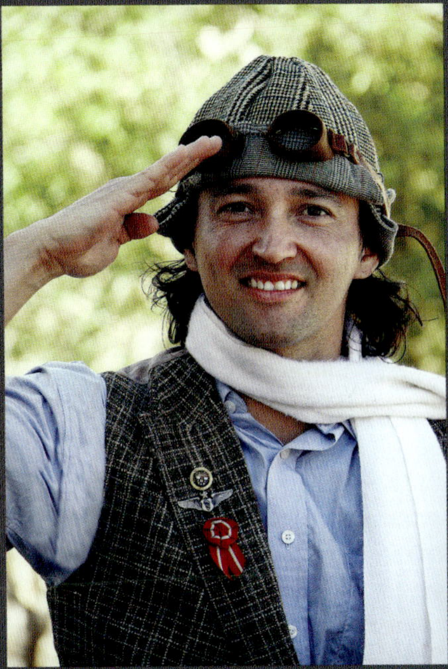

Controlled flash fill with the flash exposure at 1.3 stops less than the ambient lighting compensated for the unbalanced lighting ratio without causing discomfort to the subject, who was photographed at a community event.

It can also be useful to know how your pictures will be used; will they be published in a newsletter, posted on a website or displayed in the club's meeting rooms? Different applications will have different requirements.

When preparing for a shoot, make sure you're wearing comfortable shoes and dress in neutral colours that won't attract attention. You want to blend into the background, rather than attracting attention.

Action shots at an event are far more interesting than static shots of people posing – although these bland, on-camera flash pictures are the ones that are easiest to take. Aim to make your photos a cut above the average by recording subjects when they are interacting with others or engaged in a relevant activity.

Flash shots of people in a large room won't reveal much besides the number of people that attended. Small groups or individuals are more interesting so it's worth approaching them to have a chat before taking the photo. Make sure you're ready to take a shot when something interesting happens but, above all, avoid photographing people while they are eating.

Shooting RAW+JPEG pairs is recommended, particularly when you're working in low light levels as this gives you the best chance to correct under-exposed and over-exposed images with minimal risk of introducing noise.

Useful links

Follow the light
www.bit.ly/3ITo5ZV

Event and festival photography
www.bit.ly/3LTzKT3

Rockin' all over the world
www.bit.ly/3GyGvZ7

See more ***Photo Review*** pocket guides at **www.photoreview.com.au/guides**

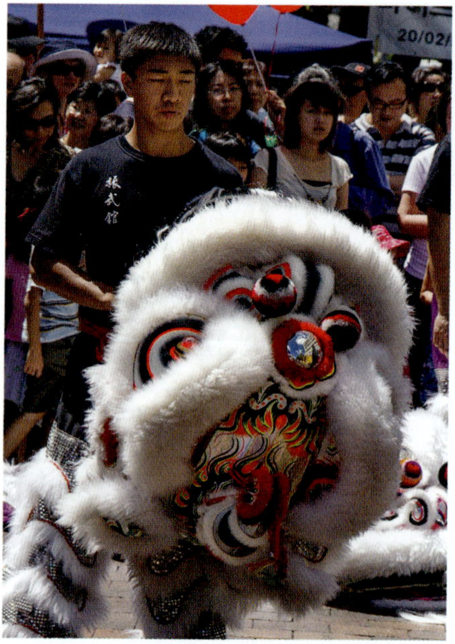

Action shots are more interesting than static, posed photographs. Capturing a backlit subject in motion can challenge your shooting skills – as well as your timing.